GOOD · OLD · DAYS®

The Best Years of Our Lives™

Backyard Wedding by John Falter © 1950 SEPS: Licensed by Curtis Publishing

Edited by Ken and Janice Tate

HOUSE of
WHITE
BIRCHES
PUBLISHERS
SINCE 1947

The Best Years of Our Lives™

Editors: Ken and Janice Tate
Managing Editor: Barb Sprunger
Editorial Assistant: Joanne Neuenschwander
Copy Supervisor: Michelle Beck,
Copy Editors: Nicki Lehman, Beverly Richardson, Läna Schurb
Assistant Editors: Marla Freeman, Marj Morgan, June Sprunger

Publishing Services Manager: Brenda Gallmeyer
Art Director: Brad Snow
Assistant Art Director: Nick Pierce
Graphic Arts Supervisor: Ronda Bechinski
Production Artists: Erin Augsburger, Pam Gregory, Shelley Muhlenkamp

Traffic Coordinator: Sandra Beres
Production Assistants: Cheryl Kempf, Jessica Tate
Photography: Tammy Christian, Carl Clark, Christena Green, Matthew Owen
Photography Stylist: Tammy Nussbaum

Chief Executive Officer: John Robinson
Publishing Director: David McKee
Marketing Director: Dan Fink
Book Marketing Director: Craig Scott
Editorial Director: Vivian Rothe

Printed in the United States of America
First Printing: 2005
Library of Congress Control Number: 2004105973
ISBN: 1-59217-053-6
Good Old Days Customer Service: (800) 829-5865

Every effort has been made to ensure the accuracy of the material in this book.
However, the publisher is not responsible for research errors or typographical mistakes in this publication.

We would like to thank the following for the art prints used in this book.

For fine-art prints and more information on the artists featured in *The Best Years of Our Lives* contact:

Curtis Publishing, Indianapolis, IN 46202, (317) 633-2070, www.curtispublishing.com

Norman Rockwell Family Trust, Antrim, N.H. 03440 (603) 588-3512

1 2 3 4 5 6 7 8 9

*D*ear Friends of the Good Old Days,

One of the most interesting lessons I have learned about life is how subjective nostalgia can be. We can laugh about that which we cried about years earlier—and vice versa. Someone said once that nostalgia is like a grammar lesson: You find the present tense and the past perfect.

So it goes when we remember that part of the Good Old Days that was the best years of our lives. It is a very subjective exercise. Still, when my dear wife Janice and I began to map out this book, we realized that the exercise was not as subjective as it first might appear.

The best years of our lives was that period of time when "The Greatest Generation" was finished with World War II and ready to start "The Boom Generation."

The Great Depression was over. The war—surely this time the one "to end all wars"—was over. It was a time to get back to work, back to school, back to sweethearts again. The economy was booming, and families were growing by leaps and bounds right alongside. Where a dark cloud had covered our land for over 15 years, now the lining was so silvery you had to shade your eyes at times.

The true accounts in this book remember those best years of our lives. From the days when Johnny Came Marching Home to The Boom Years, Janice and I have tried to capture the exuberance, the hope and, yes, some of the tears.

So, all of you who find the present tense and the past perfect, go with us back to the Good Old Days. Back to that silver lining. Back to the Best Years of Our Lives.

Ken Tate

Marriage License by Norman Rockwell © 1955 SEPS: Licensed by Curtis Publishing. Printed by permission of the Norman Rockwell Family Agency Copyright © 1955 the Norman Rockwell Family Entities.

Army, Navy & Marines by John Sheridan © 1937 SEPS

❧ Contents ☙

When Johnny Came Marching Home • 6

Milkman Meets Pieman by Stevan Dohanos © 1958 SEPS

Back to Work • 42

Motivated to Sleep by John Sheridan © 1938 SEPS

Back to School • 68

Wedding Bells • 98

The Boom Years • 132

Picking Poindexter by Richard Sargent © 1959 SEPS

Reception Line by John Falter © 1951 SEPS

Mother's Little Helpers by John Falter © 1953 SEPS

When Johnny Came Marching Home

Chapter One

It was about 1:30 a.m. EWT (Eastern War Time) on August 14, 1945. It was Tuesday. A big band remote featuring Cab Calloway and his orchestra blared on the radio live from the New Zanzibar in New York City.

Suddenly, an announcer broke in with the news we had all been awaiting: "Japan accepts Allied terms." In a matter of seconds our hopes soared like an eagle, only to come crashing down like a diving pelican. The message was quickly marked as "*not* official."

We had suffered through many premature announcements on Monday. It was interminable hours before another announcer broke in with the *official* word from the War Department and President Truman: "The war is over! The victory is won! It is over and Johnny can come marching home!"

Many historians place the end of the Great Depression at the beginning of World War II. The wartime economy was spurred by military spending on ships, planes and tanks—rifles, shells and bombs. I have said that the end of the Depression depended on what part of the country you were from. It was the late 1950s before our neck of the woods in the Ozark Mountains of southern Missouri felt a lot of the economic recovery. I guess some places were more depressed than others.

But the beginning of the best years of our lives was when Johnny (or Louis, or Bob or Steve) came marching home. We celebrated V-J Day that August 14 with even more gusto than we had V-E Day the previous May 8. In cities, sirens, whistles and church bells pierced the air, only to be dulled by the cheers of celebrants. Out in the country, where we lived, shotguns shot into the air shouted the news louder than the old Philco radio.

Now we could have closure. We could finally, completely, mourn our dead. We could bind our national wounds, and we could heal our wounded. We could weep and laugh—and we could embrace each other in the waves of emotional release.

It still might be months before Johnny burst through the door. It might be years before the economic recovery finally reached us. But the war was over! The best years of our lives had begun! We knew that when Johnny came marching home.

—Ken Tate

The Happiest Day Of Our Lives

By Audrey Carli

The news that the war with Germany had ended spread like a lovely fragrance on that May day in 1945 in Wakefield, Mich. Our town would soon welcome home the servicemen and women from their military assignments in Europe.

Whistles blew, church bells rang, and people rushed to others' homes to spread the happy report—and our family planned for the return of my uncles and cousins in the Army and Navy. Our joy hung in the air and smiles replaced worried expressions.

"Some of the men won't want to talk about the war," Mom cautioned. "Listen to what they feel free to say. Don't ask a lot of questions." My sisters, brother and I nodded in agreement.

The day was so bright and my mood so light that I called out that I was going for a walk. As I hiked, I pondered the past.

I recalled when Uncle Lloyd, my father's youngest brother, went into the Army at age 19. He rode to our home on his bicycle, the one he had purchased with his high-school paper-route money. "Here, you can have my bike now that I'll be going into the Army," he said, smiling.

"Thanks!" we kids chorused, beaming. We said we would take care of it so he could have it back when he got home again.

"Keep it," he said, smiling. "It's yours now."

We took turns riding that bike. Though we stored it in our woodshed during the frigid winter weather, the handlebars rusted to the point that Dad sawed one of them off. He worried it might break off while one of us was riding it. But we still rode it with one handlebar.

One day my sister, Myrna, failed to make a quick turn and landed in the prickly bushes by the Central School near our home. She groped her way out of the bushes and laughed. "I'm OK. Only a few scratches."

I kept pondering the past as I walked around town. I saw the fabric banners with blue stars that indicated how many family members were in the service. Soon many of them would be coming home.

Then I saw the banner with a gold star in a window, symbolizing that

In May 1945, the radio and news-paper broadcast the news about our victory in Europe. Soon after that, we got the good news that Uncle Lloyd had been liberated.

Crowds celebrate end of World War II in New York, N.Y. Circa May 7, 1945. Time Life Pictures/Getty Images

a family member had died in the war.

I thought of my friend, Sue, whose oldest brother, John, had been killed in France on D-Day in June 1944. He and Sue had exchanged V-mail letters. And sometimes, when my girlfriends and I visited at Sue's home, she shared her brother's letters with us. We all shed tears when she read John's words aloud: "I can't wait to get home to you again, little sister."

To cheer up, we stood singing around Sue's piano while she played popular songs. Soon we felt lighthearted enough to hike to the local drugstore. There, we sipped cherry Cokes and talked about fashions, music, school and boys.

We had also been serious about being patriotic, so we had collected scrap metal, toothpaste tubes and cooking fats. Many people volunteered their time to search the skies for unauthorized planes from the lookout tower by city hall.

As I walked around town, I recalled the day we got the startling news. We had just taken down our 1944 Christmas decorations when we learned that Uncle Lloyd was missing in action in Europe. Daily, we waited to hear that he had been found alive.

News finally arrived in a postcard that the Red Cross had mailed to my grandparents, Herman and Helga Johnson, from their son. Lloyd told them he was in a German prison camp.

Several weeks after the arrival of that postcard, in May 1945, the radio and newspaper broadcast the news about our victory in Europe. Soon after that, we got the good news that Uncle Lloyd had been liberated.

When I got home after my walk, Mom and Dad said that Uncle Lloyd was in an Army hospital. "He's 6 feet tall and weighed only 90 pounds when he was freed from the prison camp," they told me. But his weight and health were restored, and he rode the train home.

We met Uncle Lloyd at the train station and hugged him—hard. "So glad you're home!" we told him. He grinned, his eyes bright.

Later, we all gathered with gratitude at his welcome home party. The delicious food seemed extra tasty, the sunshine seemed brighter, and the very air seemed lighter.

We prayed a prayer of thanks for all the loved ones who were returning home to their families. Three more months would pass before V-J Day in August and the final end of the global conflict. When the rest of our family and friends returned, we would celebrate again. ❖

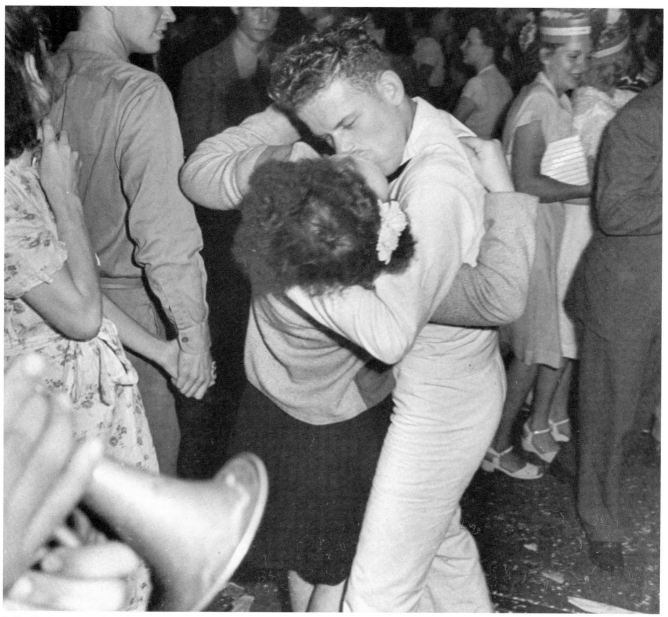

Sailor kissing pretty girl amidst crowd of revelers as they mass together during VJ day celebration surrender of Japan and the end of WWII.
Photo by Gordon Coster Circa 1945 Time Life Pictures/Getty Images

She Kept the Home Fires Burning

By Margie D. Yablonsky

*I*t was the best of times for all of us. World War II was over and peace and harmony surrounded us once again. There was no more rationing of food or gas. Mother, being alone, was raising the six of her children who remained at home. Bill, who was in the Army, and James, who was a Navy pilot, were both overseas. We displayed two gigantic stars in our front window.

Throughout all the war years, Mother kept the home fires burning—not with a fireside chat, but with strength, love and faith. She made sure she did not transmit her fears to any of us. She kept us busy writing letters and sending care packages, not only to our two brothers, but to many unknown servicemen. She always told us, "Every charitable act is a stepping-stone toward heaven." She prayed that all her heartaches, hardships and fears were but a breath away from pleasure.

In 1945, that pleasure arrived. Who could ever forget that picture of the sailor kissing the nurse in Times Square on V-J Day? Everyone, like that sailor, was in a happy frame of mind. People were friendly and showed more compassion to one another. Everything was normal again.

Mother had always planned to have a huge open house party when—and if—her boys returned home, and return they did, still youthful and unscathed. My brothers both had been engaged when they entered the service, and they married when they came home. Then the baby boom began to take hold, with Mother becoming a Grandma soon after. There was a chicken in every pot, so to speak; the housing situation was booming with the GI plan in effect, and my two brothers were able to afford beautiful homes because of it.

Opportunity was knocking on everyone's door and everyone seized the golden moment. Mother was no exception. There were more postwar brides than Carter had little pills, and Mother, being the great designer she was, opened a bridal salon and prospered, leaving behind those lean, sad days.

Soon after my brothers got settled, my mother kept her promise to have that open house party. When my brothers heard about it, they decided that we all should get together and have a party for her, to honor her for the home front duties she had performed—not in uniform, but in an apron. It was decided that every Saturday night would be a postwar party for Mother.

The idea took off like wildfire, and for many, many years, it was a tradition among our family and friends. Mother felt she did not deserve all the fuss, but she really relished every minute of it. She never lost her childlike heart.

As contentment and happiness remained, we could not believe that we had ever been unhappy and forlorn. The end of the war had put enthusiasm back in everyone's life.

I would not hesitate for a moment to go back to 1945. Those postwar Saturday-night parties are indelibly imprinted in my mind. It was a long time ago, but in memory, it is ever so near. The past is our very being, one evil less and one memory more. What was once hard to bear is sweet to remember. Mothers on the home front were just as brave as our men in the service.

Those were our Camelot years. Yes, it was the best of times. ❖

The Day The War Ended

By Dorothy Behringer

What a dusty-looking day it was! I was playing at my grandparents' farm. The air was still full of dust from a wind that had since calmed. The sun, soon to drop out of sight, looked like a faded yellow-orange ball. I could look right at it as it melted into evening. Across the coulee, the trees were so faded from the dust that I could barely see them.

I had been at Grandma's for a few days. I always had fun at my grandparents' home when I could stay by myself without my brothers and sister. I liked to have them around most of the time, but sometimes it was nice to be by myself at Grandma's house.

All we could hear on the radio were people laughing and crying, car horns blaring, and people yelling at the top of their lungs, "The war is over! The war is over!"

I was playing outside when I heard the bells. It sounded like all the bells were ringing in the town some 4 miles from us. When they kept ringing and ringing without letup, I ran into the house to tell Grandma to come and listen. "Child, that must be the church bells you are hearing," she said.

"No, no," I protested, "they don't stop at all." When I wouldn't stop pestering her, she finally shook her head and came outdoors with me.

She listened to the bells for some time and then said, "I wonder … I just wonder."

She went into the house with me at her heels. She quickly turned on the radio and listened to the news program, which seemed to be blasting away with more bells and shouting. The only thing we could understand was "The war is over! The war is over!"

It was May 8, 1945, and the war with Germany was over. All we could hear on the radio were people laughing and crying, car horns blaring, and people yelling at the top of their lungs, "The war is over! The war is over!"

I remember so well how Grandma said over and over, "Thank God, now our boys can come home," as tears ran down her face. She just seemed to glide over the floors as she finished her housework.

In the following days, the radio was a noisy madhouse. It was hard to understand what the newsmen were saying. Most of the time, all one could hear was "The war is over! It's finally over!" If it wasn't yelling, it was patriotic songs, played over and over, with voices in the background yelling, "Our boys are coming home!"

The whole world seemed excited for many days and weeks. The bells kept ringing, the yelling continued, and the horns blared away, day and night. Everyone wore a smile; you could hear their happiness whenever they spoke.

I still remember that dusty day. It was so warm, and one could see only a little distance because of all that dust in the air. It was as if it surrounded us wherever we went. But it was those bells that I still hear, as if it were yesterday—so faint at first, then louder and louder as many more bells joined in the ringing.

It was a wonderful sound, as if heaven had opened its doors to let the bells peal down to us here on earth. Thank God, the war was over. ❖

People eagerly reading New York World-Telegram newspapers with the headline NAZIS GIVE UP/SURRENDER TO ALLIES AND RUSSIA ANNOUNCED, at newsstand in Times Square as people gather for massive end to war in Europe celebration. Photo by Andreas Feining. Circa May 1945. Time Life Pictures/Getty Images

Daddy's Return To Bootie Camp

By Doris Davis

*L*oren, my husband, served three and one-half years in the Air Force during World War II. None of his military service was overseas, and I was able to be near him much of the time. That period enriched our lives in many ways. We traveled to places we wouldn't otherwise have gone, adjusting to new situations with each move. But our greatest military-created blessing came after the war ended.

Like many other young Army wives in mid-1945, I was back in the home of my parents. The future was full of uncertainties. Would Loren be sent overseas? If he was, would he return? If he didn't return, how would I survive without him? We had 2-year-old John and I was pregnant again. If he returned wounded, what would we do? These were concerns probably shared by most Army wives.

We didn't begrudge the years of Loren's military service. It was part of the responsibility that accompanied the blessing of being an American. He went where he was sent and did what he was ordered to do. We accepted this as part of our duty as American citizens. However, our lives were not our own. We longed for the freedom to choose where we would live and the opportunity to fulfill our dreams.

> *Like many other young Army wives in mid-1945, I was back in the home of my parents. The future was full of uncertainties.*

Loren had grown up on a farm, and he wanted his own land. I wanted five children and the opportunity to rear them as we chose. In the military, none of these freedoms were ours.

Then the war ended! Loren was coming home! We could finally have some control over our lives!

Not long after his discharge, we bought a farm near Yale, Okla., where my parents lived. We felt that we were entering paradise. We were together in our own home—finally free to turn our dreams into reality.

One day after we had moved, I stood outside our tiny four-room house and watched smoke rise from our brick chimney. I was almost overcome with gratitude. "Thank you, God," I whispered.

By today's standards, our little frame house was not a picture of

paradise. Its thin walls were not insulated—and we had moved into it in December! Each day, Loren cut wood for our heating stove. There was no indoor bathroom, so a beaten path led from the back door to a small frame building some 125 feet distant. The house didn't have running water, so we carried water from the well. Instead of turning on a faucet to get drinking water, we dipped it from a wooden bucket on the kitchen counter. Since we didn't have electricity, kerosene lamps lit the house after dark.

But these inconveniences were unimportant compared with the wonders that we enjoyed. I tingled with joy and gratitude. The war was over, Loren was safe, we were together with our children in our own home, and the future looked full of satisfying possibilities.

We were so isolated that our farm seemed like an island. And that's exactly what I wanted. Later we would become integrated with society again, but for now, we choose limited outside contacts—church on Sundays, activities with my parents, and an occasional shopping trip.

Our new life taught us much. We learned that some of our ideas weren't practical, so we worked out alternatives. For one thing, Loren had grown up working with registered Jersey cows, and he had planned to make our living with milk cows. This plan was discarded, and he changed to beef cattle. He also learned the

One day after we had moved, I stood outside our tiny four-room house and watched smoke rise from our brick chimney. I was almost overcome with gratitude. "Thank you, God," I whispered.

daunting challenge of being a fulltime husband and father, with the responsibility of caring for his family.

I learned to work. My day began early in the morning and lasted until after dark—a new experience for a soft town girl. I learned to cook on a wood-burning stove. I learned to use a pressure cooker, preparing food for the winter by canning the vegetables Loren raised in the garden. I learned that wild poke and lamb's-quarter make good eating. I learned the satisfaction of achieving by working.

We had the three additional children that I'd dreamed of, and I learned the joy of loving them, of doing things with them, playing with them, reading to them, and teaching them. We had little money, but we both learned that little is needed for a good life. Our first five years after the war were filled with learning experiences and achievements.

Now, almost 60 years later, looking back at our first postwar years, they sound incredibly hard. But they didn't seem difficult at the time. I didn't long for the conveniences and physical comforts that now are considered necessary. I was in heaven. We valued our new life, especially because of the few years when we were without the freedom we'd found on our Oklahoma farm. This appreciation was a surprise gift from the military. ❖

Christmas 1944

By Kate Hartnell Stobbe

Longevity assures many happy memories to recall—some happier than others. The memory I'll relate brings back that of my happiest Christmas ever. The year was 1944.

In March 1941, I got a job as a cafeteria manager at Curtiss-Wright in St. Louis County, where AT-6 trainer-fighter planes were being built. Within weeks, a certain young man in Department 25 became the light of my life. We were married within a year in a simple church ceremony.

We shared the goal of playing a more active part in our country's defense during World War II. This goal led us to enlist in the Army Air Corps. After months of specialized training, Tom became an engineer on the nine-man crew of a B-24 bomber. They were shipped to London, where they accomplished 35 bombing missions over Germany. In the meantime, as a member of the Women in the Air Force (WAF), I was stationed in Chester, England, as "girl Friday" to a highly respected general.

Furloughs found us visiting well-known sites in London and the English countryside. Tom's crew often came with us. Meeting and knowing these men gave me much confidence as I witnessed their mutual respect for each other, their positive attitude and kinship loyalty. I also corresponded with their wives or parents to keep them posted as to the crew's "state of the union," as we called our writings.

Crew of the B-24 bomber, Sadie Mae.

It was on their 35th mission, in April 1944, that the *Sadie Mae,* the christened name of their bomber, was reported missing in action somewhere over Nauen, Germany, just west of Berlin. Months of tearful, prayerful waiting ensued.

That November, after receiving this heartbreaking news, I was flown

back to the States to await the arrival of our first child, due shortly before Christmas. I settled in Kansas City, Mo., where I rented a small apartment and began shopping for the necessities, along with Christmas decorations. A small tabletop tree gave our "home" a festive, holiday appearance. Once I got back, I had contacted the families of the *Sadie Mae's* crew through phone calls, pictures and several visits. Each night, and during many daylight hours, I prayed for the crew and their families.

Faith was my watchword as I waited hopefully for news of the *Sadie Mae* and her men. I often spoke to my unborn child of his heavenly Father who would watch over him if his earthly father couldn't be with him, and of the Baby Jesus, whose birth we would soon celebrate.

Twelve days before Christmas, Gerald Lee came into the world. We came home from the hospital in time to light our small tree and listen to joyous carols playing on the local radio station.

Just before 7 p.m. on Christmas Eve, after Gerald's feeding, as I knelt beside his crib and listened to his contented gurgles, a soft rap on our apartment door roused me. An Air Force major stood in the doorway. He smiled broadly and said, "I have some news for you, Mrs. S." Peeking from around the major's back was my husband.

A happy Christmas? You can believe it—and even more so when I learned that the entire crew had been transported to their respective homes in time for Christmas. All were in good health, although they had been held in German prison camps where they had performed hard labor and endured constant interrogation for many months.

I hadn't known the major previously, but I learned that he had accompanied the crew on that luckless mission to complete a comparison report. He wasn't able to make connections to his home in Seattle for that day, but had called his family to let them know of his safe arrival in the States.

Sharing such a mutual bond, we three talked all night and found much happiness just being together, safe and free. Then Christmas morning dawned, hallowed and bright. The new father found moments to become acquainted with his baby son. And after breakfast, the major took a cab to Union Station to catch his train and enjoy a much-anticipated reunion with his loved ones in Washington.

Many Christmases have gone by, but the holiday of 1944 lives in my mind as the happiest ever.

At triennial reunions, we often fly off into "the wild blue yonder" in memory with crewmates and their families as we recall the *Sadie Mae*. We thank God for the safe return of her crew. And, prayerfully, we remember all the veterans who assured the preservation of our nation's ongoing freedom. ❖

Barn Dance by Mead Schaeffer © 1944 SEPS: Licensed by Curtis Publishing

Renewing Reunions

By Janice Julius

*M*y father's family has had family reunions for almost 70 years. The turnout has been better in some years than others, but the first summer after World War II, almost every family was represented. All our uncles and cousins were back from the war. Food wasn't rationed anymore. Gas and tires were becoming more widely available. Spirits were high.

My Aunt Pearl had always been in charge of the coffee, but now it wasn't rationed. She had two oversized blue campfire pots going all day. You could smell the aroma all over the forest preserve. She liked to put a crushed egg, shell and all, into a cloth bag with the coffee grounds. She said it made the coffee clear of settlings. Our family members are great coffee lovers, so gathering around the coffeepot seemed a natural thing to do, waiting for that first cup.

In 1947 the reunion was held in Kilbuck Forest Preserve, south of Rockford, Ill. It was an ideal spot, with big trees creating shade and the Kilbuck Creek flowing through it into the Kiswaukee River. We had reserved the big shelter house. Signs were posted everywhere, marking the way to our site.

Every time a car drove up, everyone who had already arrived became the welcoming committee. Hugs and kisses greeted the returning soldiers, but there were also tears of joy. Some of us stood in line to hug our favorite cousin, who had been taken to Japan as a prisoner of war. He was very thin from his ordeal, but to us he looked like a million dollars. No one asked about war experiences. This was a day of thanksgiving and happiness.

Three long picnic tables were arranged in the middle of the shelter house. It looked like a Roman banquet with all the potluck dishes. There was Aunt Dorothy's pickled herring and my mom's pies that melted in your mouth. Everyone brought her best concoction.

There were about 20 other picnic tables along the sides. Each family put out a tablecloth and table service to reserve their table for the day. We were in an open-air shelter house, but even rain couldn't have dampened this day. When we thought almost everyone was there, my dad stood to say grace, thanking God for returning all of our service members to us. Everyone cheered for the military guys to go first down the buffet line.

Announcements were made—who was the oldest, who was the youngest, who had the biggest family, who had made the longest journey to get there. The day was filled with horseshoe contests, with husband-and-wife teams competing against each other, kids against kids, etc. And of course, there was the dishwashing brigade. This was before paper plates and disposable table service was common. Most of the women brought their dishpans, and with the pump right outside the shelter house, washing up offered another opportunity to gossip and catch up on family news.

As dusk fell, the guitars and banjos came out. Exhausted from the day's games, we settled in for music and singing. All of my father's nine siblings could play at least one musical instrument. Music makes the heart light. My grandfather's brothers did the old soft-shoe. They threw sand on the concrete floor and their tapping made a rhythmic sound.

> *Every time a car drove up, everyone who had already arrived became the welcoming committee. Hugs and kisses greeted the returning soldiers, but there were also tears of joy.*

My father played the spoons. Placing two teaspoons back to back, he slapped them against his hands, knees and anything near him. He really played the bass fiddle, but there was no fiddle in the park that day.

Most of my uncles played guitars and banjos. Uncle Clyde played his mandolin. Even the kids settled down to listen. We harmonized to *Down By the Old Mill Stream*. My dad's three sisters tap-danced and performed the buck-and-wing, a complicated tap step, much to everyone's surprise.

Almost everyone had a camera. Good old Aunt Pearl had an old-fashioned Brownie box camera. It was old even back then, but it took great pictures. Everyone wanted photos of all the veterans and their immediate families. We all got tired of posing for pictures. But who knew when so many of us would be together again?

We had to be out of the forest preserve by 10 o'clock that evening. It was getting late, but many lingered, not wanting the day to end. The goodbyes brought tears again, as everyone promised to come next year. ❖

The dishwashing brigade. Front (left to right): Aunt Millie, me, Aunt Rosilee, my sister, Marylou; back (left to right): Aunt Eva, my mom, Mrs. Carlson, Aunt Dorothy, and Aunt Ruth.

The Prom

By Helen Patton Gray

orld War II had ended a few months before my junior-senior prom. The day peace was declared, my parents and I were away from our home in Kansas City, Mo., enjoying a day at our favorite fishing hole. We had heard that the end was near, and the news finally reached us by way of our portable radio. We cheered and shed tears of joy when we learned that it was finally over, that the servicemen would be returning, and that our family would be whole again.

When we arrived back in town from our fishing trip, there were still street celebrations going on all over town. I begged to join them, but Mom and Dad knew that they were a little too wild for a 16-year-old girl.

I missed my two older brothers. Dick was an Army captain, and Jack was a "swabby"—seaman first class—in the Navy. A few of the students from Bishop Hogan High, the small school I attended, had joined the ranks as well. Now they would all be home soon.

There were other things for me to do while waiting. One was to prepare for my high-school prom. I was on the decorating committee, lending a hand in transforming our gymnasium into "An Evening in Paris." We rounded up crepe paper, which was a bit scarce during wartime, and sparkle dust to glue to cardboard stars. One of the committee members was able to borrow a ballroom fixture with a 2-foot-diameter mirrored

Front cover of Helen Patton Gray's prom book from the junior-senior prom held at the Bishop Hogan High School on Friday evening, May 3, 1946.

rotating sphere. It would hang from the ceiling over the dance floor to create a lighthearted Parisian atmosphere as it cast shadows and lights on the auditorium. We thought it was elegant and would surely make it a night to remember for everyone.

I had a problem, however. Girls outnumbered boys three to one at Hogan High, and I did not have a date for the prom. Although I wasn't alone in that category, I felt sad that even after helping decorate, spending hours after school to make it a success, I would not be attending the prom. Several of my close friends were in the same spot.

Because of the boy shortage, we were allowed to invite escorts from other schools. But that didn't help me because I had no boyfriends anywhere. I didn't date until after my high-school graduation.

Then, about two weeks before prom night, my brother Jack arrived home from the Navy. Seeing his little sister in a jam, he offered to be my date for the evening. A few of my friends came with their newly discharged brothers, also.

When some of the girls who had teenage dates heard that my big brother was going to be my escort, they snickered and thought it was crazy to bring a brother to a prom. When I tried to solicit signups for my dance card, I ended up with several blanks the day before the prom. I dreaded the thought of Jack and me sitting on the sidelines or not changing partners while others were having fun.

However, the night of the prom finally came. Jack brought me a beautiful corsage of pink roses to wear on my formal, and we made our grand entrance, me in my pretty chiffon dress and Jack in his Navy attire. Everyone paid attention! Jack was handsome and a terrific dancer. His jitterbug turned heads and made quite a stir. When word got out that he was my brother and available for some of the dances, my card was quickly filled, and I had to turn down some latecomers who were begging to have just one dance with Jack. I'll never forget that night and my wonderful brother who came to my rescue.

As I was going through some memorabilia recently, I came across my prom card from 1946. I smiled like Mona Lisa and was reminded of how nice it is to have big brothers. To this day, Jack is considered handsome; he has an overflowing heart, and can still "cut the rug"—but at a moderate tempo, due to his pacemaker. ❖

> *The night of the prom finally came. Jack brought me a beautiful corsage of pink roses to wear on my formal, and we made our grand entrance, me in my pretty chiffon dress and Jack in his Navy attire.*

JUNIOR-SENIOR PROM
BISHOP HOGAN HIGH
SCHOOL

★ ★ ★

Dutch Holland's Orchestra

★ ★ ★

Friday Evening, May 3, 1946

Kansas City, Missouri

Inside front page of Helen's prom book.

norman
rockwell

An About Face

By Lee Hill-Nelson

*D*usk had settled when the phone rang. It was my friend Joe, who was in sick bay, recuperating from the flu.

"Hey, Tex," he said, "bring my buddy and me a malted milk from Ship's Store. Chow was no good tonight."

I told him I'd be right over.

I quickly dressed in my uniform. Though the war was over, I had reenlisted for another six months in the U.S. Navy WAVES. We dressed in full uniform when we left the barracks, even if we were going someplace on base close by.

I looked in the mirror, straightened my shoulders, and reminded myself that I was in the greatest Navy in the world. Outside, the Wasatch Mountains outlined the sky. As I looked across the peaceful Utah valley, I felt happy and at peace.

The workers in Ship's Store made good malted milks—thick, with lots of ice cream, malt and whole milk, beaten until foamy, all for 25 cents. I bought two and headed for sick bay.

"This is my buddy, Franz," said Joe as he motioned to the bed next to him. My gaze wandered briefly around sick bay. It was almost empty. The few patients who were there wore Navy hospital pajamas and in that way looked alike.

I sat down and listened as the two military men continued talking. Joe, with his Chicago brogue, and Franz, in German-accented English.

"We're sure hungry for those malts," Franz said. I turned my head sharply at the sound of Franz's heavy German accent and stared at him. He was German, a prisoner of war—the *enemy.* Why had Joe asked me to bring a malt to a Nazi?

I didn't want to give him the malted milk, but because Joe had asked me, I handed it to Franz. When he smiled, I forced a smile in return.

It was early 1946. Prisoners of war had been brought to the Naval Supply Depot at Clearfield, Utah. Tight security prevailed. Shore Patrols, wearing guns and holsters, guarded them. Posted rules stated that only authorized personnel were to talk with the prisoners, but no rules kept us from seeing and observing them.

Like a regimental review in the early mornings and late afternoons, they marched the famous goose-step to and from work, keeping perfect lines and eyes straight ahead. They whistled tunes such as *Beer Barrel Polka* and *Lilli Marlene.* Sometimes one of them spat on the ground, as if showing, we thought, his feelings toward us Americans.

Some prisoners looked younger than 18 years of age; others were men in their late 30s or early 40s. We assumed many in-betweens had met death in the war.

At Clearfield, the prisoners cared for the grounds, making the grass green and flowers bloom like never before. Hard work seemed to fit them.

It seemed strange to me that with all the rules on the base, Joe and Franz could be friends in the hospital. Why, I wondered again, had Joe asked me to bring a malted milk to an enemy?

I sat down and listened as the two military men continued talking. Joe, with his Chicago brogue, and Franz, in German-accented English, spoke easily and good-naturedly, discussing their homes and families, their governments and the war. I marveled at Joe's willingness to accept Franz as a friend, and his treatment of Franz gradually eased my defense. I studied Franz carefully.

Lee Hill-Nelson, U.S. Navy Waves, 1944.

Noting his blond hair and sad blue eyes, I could see he was young, probably about the age of my youngest brother. The same age as my youngest brother! The comparison hit me like a slap in the face. My little brother was at home in high school, and this boy had just come out of combat as a prisoner of war!

"I'm glad to be in Clearfield," Franz said.

"Some of my friends had to go to Idaho to pick beets. I hope President Truman will let us go home soon."

He said that he wanted to go home! I began to do an about-face. I realized that Franz was a real person, as real as Joe or my little brother! He wanted to be at home with his family just as much as we did. He, too, had fought in a war he had not asked for.

Joe and Franz were patients together in sick bay for a few more days. Now, in the evenings, after work, I visited two friends instead of one. We laughed together, and we shared jokes and stories about families and homes in Texas, Chicago and Germany. We looked forward to a world again at peace.

Franz went back to the prisoner-of-war group when he left sick bay. Sometimes I caught a glimpse of him marching by. Joe was discharged and went home to Chicago. All WAVES at Clearfield were transferred to San Francisco, where I served for three more months before going home to Texas.

When Franz returned to Germany, I like to think that he remembered the sailor who, without hesitation, treated him with brotherly love, and the WAVE who, though it took awhile, did an about-face. ❖

My Wartime Buddy

By Dorothy M. Stanaitis

When Uncle Dave came home from the war, he brought a new member of the family back with him. No, it wasn't a war bride. He and Aunt Rose had been married before he left Philadelphia for the service in the Merchant Marine.

Aunt Rose was a tall, elegant blonde with a witty personality and an endless supply of funny stories. I always looked forward to her visits when we would all sit in the living room of our little city row house and talk and laugh.

If my mother had to change the baby or answer the phone, Aunt Rose would play with me until she returned. I especially remember the day she joined me on the floor to color in the new Pinocchio coloring book that she had brought. I chose the page with the picture of Figaro, the cat. Aunt Rose didn't care much for cats, so she picked Cleo, the goldfish, to color. I was amazed at the way she used those terrible wartime crayons that usually softened and bent in my hands. Her Cleo was a light golden orange, and the bubbles coming from Cleo's mouth were pastel pink, blue and green. My poor Figaro was a fairly gruesome black crayon scribble that wavered in intensity and often went outside the lines.

I wondered why such a fun-loving aunt wasn't interested in our cat. He was an amusing creature, and put up with all sorts of petting and playing. But Aunt Rose did love playing with my baby brother and often spoke about the family she would have someday when Uncle Dave returned.

Still, as much as I enjoyed Aunt Rose's visits, it made me uneasy when, thinking I was absorbed in playing, she would start whispering to my mother and father. I could tell by their expressions that something serious was being discussed. I knew better

than to ask about it for fear of being sent outside to play. But I was sure that the whispering was about Uncle Dave, and it made me worry. I always felt better when the whispering stopped and Aunt Rose joined me in playing while my mother made coffee for the grownups and poured milk for me. She often served her famous lemon meringue pie that Uncle Dave loved so much.

Then came the happy day when the whispering stopped for good and the laughing and planning began. Uncle Dave was on his way home. Aunt Rose hugged me extra tight and said that he was bringing nice surprises for all of us.

Well, we certainly were surprised when, after we opened the pretty gifts he had for us, he told us about the special package he had brought home. I still remember the look on my mother's face as she sat holding the beautiful cameo pin Uncle Dave had given her.

"A cat!" she exclaimed. "Where did you get a cat?"

Well, it seemed that when Uncle Dave had been stationed in England, a solid black Persian cat had been seen prowling around the area for a few days. It seemed lost and lonely, and some of the Merchant Marines began feeding it. Then, on the terrible night of an air raid, as Uncle Dave and his friends ran for shelter, he saw the cat, frightened and confused, crouched in terror near the air-raid shelter entrance. Almost without thinking, Uncle Dave scooped up the terrified animal and took it into the shelter with him. They huddled together all night until the all-clear sounded.

By then, the cat had become attached to Uncle Dave. It followed him until Uncle Dave picked him up again and smuggled him into his quarters. Since the cat was jet black and Uncle Dave had found him during a blackout, naming him was easy. The cat became Blackie.

Almost without thinking, Uncle Dave scooped up the terrified animal and took it into the shelter with him. They huddled together all night until the all-clear sounded.

With the help of his friends—and perhaps the blind eye of his officers—Uncle Dave kept Blackie and brought him all the way home to America.

But there was a problem. Aunt Rose didn't care for cats because she was allergic to them. Her eyes became red, watery and itchy. She would sneeze and cough if the cat came too close. Also, housing was in short supply in Philadelphia after the war, and few apartments would rent to pet owners. The cat would have to go.

Uncle Dave couldn't bear to send Blackie away after all they had been through together, so he made a plan. We were all cat lovers at our house. He would give his pet to us; then he could see it whenever he came to visit.

My parents were speechless, but what could they do? The only question that remained was whether our cat would accept the newcomer.

When Uncle Dave brought Blackie to our house, it was love at first sight. The beautiful war refugee curled up on my mother's lap and began purring. My father, who worked in a meat market, had Blackie following him—or the delicious aroma of his shoes—all around the house. Our original cat didn't even seem to notice the newcomer. When the neighbors came to see our new cat, they thought there were two; the Persian cat's tail, curled up around him as he slept, looked like a little kitten. Blackie had found a new home.

Soon Aunt Rose and Uncle Dave found a new home, too. Within a year they had a new apartment and a new baby, and they had opened a new diner on the outskirts of the city.

Every day, Uncle Dave would come to our house to pick up the lemon meringue pies that my mother baked for his diner, and to visit with his old wartime buddy, Blackie, the cat. ❖

Brother Jim

By Bob Griggs

It was 1944. I was 13 and a brand-new freshman at U.S. Grant High School in Portland, Ore., and I was almost late for my first-period class. I ran around the corner and right into our student body president. Books flew everywhere.

Jimmy Faubion, all of 18 years old himself, laughed, helped me pick up my books, and said, "On your way, youngster, don't be late." Jimmy could say something like that, and with him it was perfectly natural. I made it to my class on time with the light of hero worship shining in my eyes.

Jim was tall and good-looking, with a shock of black hair and a ready smile that had the girls languishing over him. Even then, I never heard of anybody who didn't like him. He made top grades and because he got along well with the teachers and principal, he was probably the best student body president the school ever had. Being the oldest in my family, I immediately cast him as the big brother I never had. Somehow he found out my name, and he never failed to say "Hello" when we passed in the halls.

Graduation was in June. To no one's surprise, right after graduation, Jimmy joined the Marines. We were at war, and he wanted to do his part.

Graduation was in June. To no one's surprise, right after graduation, Jimmy joined the Marines. We were at war, and he wanted to do his part.

He completed his training and, in due course, ended up taking part in the Marine attack on the island of Okinawa. But Jimmy made it only a short way up the beach before he was hit by a Japanese bullet. It took him in the back, severing his spinal cord just above the hips, and doing massive internal damage.

He lay on the beach, paralyzed and semiconscious, for more than two days. When I asked him later what he remembered about that time, he said, "I was trying to make myself move enough so somebody would know I was alive."

Somehow, through sheer force of will, he did. The medics got to him and he was evacuated to a hospital ship where the doctors managed to stabilize his injuries. Nothing could be done about the severed spinal cord or the kidney he'd lost, or the damage to the remaining one.

His troubles weren't over, either. The tremendous number of injured stretched the available medical resources to the maximum, and because he couldn't get the therapy he needed, he developed bedsores.

Gangrene set in, and he had to have both legs amputated just below the hips.

He and many others were sent back to the States. His prognosis was not good, and the pain and physical suffering he endured must have been intense. But his incredible will triumphed, and he lived.

We students, of course, heard about his injuries. I knew that he was in a veterans' hospital somewhere, but that's all we knew, and no one could tell us more.

I met Jimmy again in 1947. I was a senior by then, and my drama teacher sent several of us boys down to the Portland Civic Theater to do walk-ons in a production of Shakespeare's *The Merchant of Venice*. We were all pretty excited, but I was the most excited of all—for there, sitting in his wheelchair, semi-discharged from the veterans' hospital, was James Blair Faubion. He had been active in the theater during high school and now he was back to play one of Portia's suitors, the Prince of Aragon.

And how did Jimmy do this in a wheelchair? He didn't. He was carried onto the stage in a sedan chair, and what an elegant fop he was! Too languid to even rise from the chair, he was a hit. I was the back chair bearer. Could anything have been better? My hero, and I got to help carry him onto the stage!

But it *did* get better. Jimmy had a Chevrolet car fitted with hand controls, and I found out that I lived only a short distance from his house. Jimmy started giving me lifts to and from the theater. It worked out well for him, too, since I could help him with his wheelchair and generally make it easier for him to get around.

Scene from Shakespear's The Merchant of Venice given in 1947 at the Portland Civic Theater, Portland, Oregan. Jimmy Faubion who played one of Portia's suitors, the Prince of Aragon, is sitting in the chair. Author Bob Griggs is standing in the center with arms folded.

It wasn't long before he and several other former-servicemen-turned-actors in the play adopted me as sort of kid brother. I got to hang out with them and listen to their stories of their experiences in the war.

Jimmy had enrolled in Reed College in Portland to study playwriting. How he managed to do this and still find time to be onstage in two more plays with his physical limitations was amazing. But he was determined to lead as normal a life as possible. I had a job at the theater by this time, as well as roles in the two other plays he was in, and so I got to see a lot of him. I helped out as much as I could.

He played the stage manager in Thornton Wilder's *Our Town* in his wheelchair and did an incredible, moving job.

We arrived at the cast party after the play, and I pushed him into the house in his chair. Jimmy had managed to sweet-talk my mother, who worked in a department store, into loaning him two transparent plastic leg forms for displaying stockings. He fitted them with a pair of argyle socks and highly polished brogues and installed them inside his pant legs. No one seemed to notice until, in the midst of telling a story, he casually reached down, pulled up his pant leg and started to scratch. There was dead silence. At the startled looks on so many faces, Jimmy started laughing so hard that he almost fell out of his wheelchair. The rest finally joined in the laughter. It was one of many wonderful jokes he played.

There were no kidney transplants then, and no dialysis, and Jimmy was spending more and more time up at the veterans' hospital. He never let on as to how sick he really was, but I think some of us knew that he was dying. It was just a matter of time.

I had been over to see him a day or so before it happened. His color wasn't good, but he was wearing his cheerful face, and so I pretended along with him that he was OK.

Jimmy died on June 12, 1949. Later his mother told us that he had been in his room that day, in his special bed. As she was going down the hall, she heard him call out to her. "I'm busy, Jimmy," she answered.

"You've got to come now, Mom," he said. "I'm dying." His mother had been an Army nurse in World War II. She didn't need a second look to know that it was true, and she burst into tears.

"Don't cry, Mom," Jimmy said. "It's the most wonderful thing that's ever happened to me. I just wish I could write down what it's like." And then he did a particularly Jimmy

He took her hand and began to recite the "To be or not to be" speech from Hamlet, which he loved to perform as an old, quavering-voiced, Shakespearean actor.

thing. He took her hand and began to recite the "To be or not to be" speech from *Hamlet,* which he loved to perform as an old, quavering-voiced, Shakespearean actor. Halfway through, he shifted to his normal voice. Then he finished the speech, squeezed her hand, smiled and was gone.

His funeral was really a celebration. Dozens of his friends were there, laughing and crying and hugging each other and telling wonderful Jimmy stories. One of his old girl-friends said that she could just see Jimmy looking down and saying, "Not a bad crowd for an opening night!"

I could hardly bear it at the time because I thought I'd lost a big brother, a mentor, and especially a friend. I discovered that I hadn't, though, because I know now that some of the best lessons I learned about growing up I got from this brilliant, witty, generous, courageous young man. I remember him vividly to this day. ❖

Bringing Jackie Home

By Joyce Normandin

His name was John Davern, but everyone called him Jackie. People would joke that he had "the map of Ireland" on his face. He seemed tall to me, but then I was only 8 at the time. He had dark curly hair, sparkling blue eyes and a slim build.

When family and friends got together and the younger ones looked bored with all the adult talk, Jackie would say, "Hey, how about walking up to Katie's candy store and getting an ice-cream cone or a bag of penny candy?" Sometimes he would take us to the playground around the corner and push us high on the swings or help us negotiate the monkey bars.

He was the only son of a widowed mother and he was her pride and joy. Because she was very religious and devout, every Sunday morning would find him dutifully escorting her and his older sister, Rita, to church. Rita adored him.

In the Brooklyn Irish neighborhood where he grew up, he was popular and always ready for a game of stickball with "the gang," a trip to a Dodgers game or to Coney Island. He was ever willing to give someone a hand with chores or help tinker on their cars. He loved it when friends and family would get together. He knew all of those old Irish songs and joined in with his pleasant tenor. One of his favorites was *Mother McCree,* and when he sang it, he always sang it to his mother, which never failed to bring tears to her eyes.

Jackie came home on leave from basic training before being shipped overseas. There was a big party held for him, with all the relatives, neighbors and friends.

He had a lusty appetite but never seemed to gain weight, probably because he was so active in sports. He did a lot to help around the house, too. It was no surprise to find him hammering, sawing or painting. He was a demon for corned beef and cabbage and, true Irishman that he was, he could not abide a meal without potatoes. He could wreak havoc on a loaf of his mother's Irish soda bread, watercress sandwiches or his sister's homemade chicken soup.

A good student, he graduated from high school when only 17 and took a temporary job at a local market. He had decided that he wanted to be a policeman like his late father, but he knew with the war on that it was inevitable that he would be called up. So he decided to enlist. He joked that he was saving the draft board a lot of trouble.

His mother and sister cried, but they knew that most of the boys from the neighborhood were already in uniform serving their country in far-off places. Jackie was wearing an Army uniform the last time I saw him. He looked so brave and sharp. I felt so proud of him.

He had come home on leave from basic training before being shipped overseas. There was a big party held for him, with all the relatives, neighbors and friends packing their house and overflowing into the back yard and onto the front steps. They were eating from a fantastic spread to which everyone in the family had contributed. Some men pitched in for a keg of beer and pretty soon everyone was singing, laughing and dancing. Jackie didn't have a special girlfriend, but there were many who would write to him in the coming months.

After he left to go back to camp, his mother seemed lonelier and quieter. Whenever we invited her and Rita for lunch or dinner, she would remark on how much Jackie would have enjoyed that meal.

One day, I came home from school to find my mother crying. "Hurry," she said, "we are going over to Mrs. Davern's. She received a telegram that Jack was killed in action." It was 1944; Jackie had been killed at Anzio. He was only 18. It seemed unbelievable that the young, wonderful boy that I knew was not coming home again.

When we arrived at the Davern home, we found that most of his family members were already congregated there and in tears. His mother sat in a chair in the living room, dabbing at her eyes with a handkerchief. She seemed stunned by the news. Rita was trying to keep some sense of order, making coffee and setting out cups as neighbors arrived with bowls and platters of food. Everyone spoke in hushed tones.

A few days later, a funeral service was held, and the huge church appeared to have barely adequate room for all the people who attended. Jackie had been loved and liked by just about everyone. Mrs. Davern set up a small table with some photographs, a religious statue and some votive candles in her living room, next to her favorite chair, so she could glance at them often. She prayed for Jackie and for all the others who were still fighting in Europe and the Pacific.

After the war, his mother began to speak of how she would like Jackie to be "brought home" and buried in the local cemetery. Rita tried to pacify her by saying that it would be "looked into." After a friend or neighbor mentioned that it might be possible for the government to do just that, Rita spent many hours writing and visiting government and veterans organizations to see how this could be done. She would "move heaven and earth," she used to say,

A funeral service was held, and the huge church appeared to have barely adequate room for all the people who attended. Jackie had been loved and liked by just about everyone.

to accomplish this because it was her mother's dearest wish. There was some debate in the family about it, but most said the same thing: Jackie deserved to be home. It was where he was born and where he should be laid to rest. A headstone would be purchased and he would be placed next to his father in the local cemetery.

In the midst of all this debate, there came a visitor. One Sunday, when the family was just returning from church, the doorbell rang. Standing there was a young man about Jackie's age. He inquired if he had the right house. Rita invited him in and he introduced himself to her mother. "My name is Bill," he said. He explained that although he was in New York City for only a short time, he had made it his personal mission to contact Jackie's folks. He and Jackie had fought together at Anzio and other places, and they had been buddies.

Just a day or so before the battle, Bill said, he noticed Jackie saying his rosary, which he always carried. It had been a gift for his First Holy Communion. When Bill told Jack that he had not said the rosary in a long time, Jackie offered him his silver and dark blue rosary beads. Bill said he used them, and in the confusion of the invasion, forgot to return them. When he discovered that Jackie had fallen, he had kept the beads and carried them all through the rest of the war. When he returned home, he put them in a safe place and vowed that someday he would bring them to Jackie's family.

Bill lived in Ohio, and this had been his first opportunity to come to New York. He was here now on his honeymoon. He reached into his pocket, brought out the rosary beads and handed them to Mrs. Davern. It was a little bit of Jackie coming home.

Rita explained to Bill the plans to bring Jackie home again. Bill looked a bit uncomfortable. Perhaps, he suggested, they should consider that Jackie had fallen with his comrades and was buried next to them, next to buddies with whom he had been through a lot of hard fighting. "I know that if it was me," he said, "I would want to stay near those guys. As time passes on, sooner or later, people will forget that he is buried here," he explained. "But over there, he is resting in a place where he will always be remembered. It's maybe where he would want to be."

Bill stayed for coffee. Then he hugged Mrs. Davern and Rita and left.

Mrs. Davern grasped the beads and held them to her heart. After all this time, they were back where they belonged—but was Jackie where he belonged? After some discussion, it was finally decided to leave Jackie buried in Europe. "After all," Mrs. Davern said, "someday I will be buried next to my husband, so he won't be alone." She used Jackie's rosary every day for the rest of her life.

Bill was right. It was 60 years ago, in 1944, that Jackie died in Anzio. Now almost all the rest of his family and friends are gone or scattered. We went on with our lives and enjoyed the postwar prosperity that followed in what was described as the best years of our lives. No one visits the cemetery anymore or seems to remember Jackie, Rita or Mrs. Davern. My brother was only a little more than a year old when Jackie died. Today the "younger ones" are in their 60s or 70s—even older. They moved away years ago, or are gone now, too.

Rita never married, but stayed at home, taking care of her mother until she died. Mrs. Davern was buried

with Jackie's rosary beads. Rita passed away a few years later. I am about the only one left who still recalls that handsome boy with the twinkling Irish eyes who had so much promise, who wanted to be a policeman, who loved corned beef, cabbage and potatoes, who always carried his rosary. He is at rest in a far-off land, the land where he fell in battle, a young hero resting next to other heroes who were his pals. He remains in my heart and forever young in my memory. ❖

A solute to all our soldiers who died fighting for freedom during WWII. A wooden cross, a soldier's helmet, and flowers mark the grave of an American soldier who was killed in battle during the invasion of Normandy, Carentan, France. A sign posted by French civilians reads "Mort pour la France." Or "Died for France."
Photo by Himes/US Army. Circa June 17, 1944. Getty Images

Marching Songs

Many times, music was what kept us going through the tough days of World War II until Johnny came marching home.

Some of the songs made us laugh, like *Boogie Woogie Bugle Boy (of Company B)*, with music and lyrics by Don Raye and Hughie Prince. *Boogie Woogie Bugle Boy* was a big hit for the Andrews Sisters from the Abbott and Costello movie *Buck Privates* (1940).

The song almost was nixed from the film because some executives were afraid that the American public, still politically divided on the issue of the newly instituted peacetime draft, would not find the whimsical lyrics funny. Fortunately for all of us, *Boogie Woogie Bugle Boy* made it to the big screen. The wonderful song has endured now for over 60 years, including a revival recording by Bette Midler in 1972.

Boogie Woogie Bugle Boy

He was a famous trumpet man from out
   Chicago way.
He had a boogie style that no one else could play.
He was the top man at his craft,
But then his number came up and he was gone
   with the draft.
He's in the Army now. He's blowin' reveille.
He's the boogie woogie bugle boy of Company B.

They made him blow a bugle for his Uncle Sam.
It really brought him down because he could
   not jam.
The captain seemed to understand,
Because the next day the cap' went out and
   drafted the band.
And now the company jumps when he
   plays reveille.
He's the boogie woogie bugle boy of Company B.

A root, a toot, a toodlie-a-da-toot.
He blows it eight to the bar in boogie rhythm.
He can't blow a note unless a bass and guitar
Is playin' with him.
And the company jumps when he plays reveille.
He's the boogie woogie bugle boy of Company B.
He puts the boys to sleep with boogie every night,
And wakes 'em up the same way in the
   early bright.
They clap their hands and stamp their feet,
'cause they know how it goes when someone
   gives him a beat.
Woah, woah, he wakes 'em up when he
   plays reveille.
The boogie woogie bugle boy of Company B.

A root, a toot, a toodli-a-da to toot toot toot
He's blowin' eight to the bar.
Yeah, he can't blow a note if a bass and guitar
Isn't, woah, with him.
And the company jumps when he plays reveille.
He's the boogie woogie bugle boy of Company B.

Other songs, like *I'll Be Seeing You* tugged at our heartstrings as we waited desperately to be united with wives and sweethearts.

The lyrics by Sammy Fain and Irving Kahal were bittersweet; they reminded us that the old familiar places, half a continent or half a world away, were waiting for the day when the war would end and the best years of our lives could finally begin.

I'll Be Seeing You

I'll be seeing you
In all the old familiar places
That this heart of mine embraces
All day through

In that small cafe
The park across the way
The children's carousel
The chestnut trees, the wishing well

I'll be seeing you
In every lovely summer's day
In everything that's light and gay
I'll always think of you that way.

I'll find you in the mornin' sun
And when the night is new
I'll be looking at the moon
But I'll be seeing you.

I'll be seeing you
In all the old familiar places
That this heart of mine embraces
All day through.

I'll find you in the mornin' sun
And when the night is new
I'll be looking at the moon
But I'll be seeing you.

Then there was *Don't Sit Under the Apple Tree (With Anyone Else But Me)*, written and composed by Lew Brown, Charles Tobias and Sam H. Stept.

This classic, fun song was written like a letter from a soldier to his girl back home and then faithful her response back to him, promising to "be true 'til you come marchin' home."

Don't Sit Under the Apple Tree
Male Vocal:
Don't sit under the apple tree with anyone else
    but me,
Anyone else but me, anyone else but me—
    no, no, no.
Don't sit under the apple tree with anyone else
    but me,
'Til I come marchin' home.

Don't go walkin' down Lovers' Lane with
    anyone else but me,
Anyone else but me, anyone else but me—
    no, no, no.
Don't go walkin' down Lovers' Lane with any-
    one else but me,
'Til I come marchin' home.

I just got word from a guy who heard
From the guy next door to me.
The girl he met just loves to pet,
And it fits you to a tee.
So, Don't sit under the apple tree with anyone
    else but me
'Til I come marchin' home.

Female Vocal:
Don't give out with those lips of yours to any-
    one else but me
Anyone else but me, anyone else but me—
    no, no, no.
Watch those girls on foreign shores; you'll have
    to report to me
When you come marchin' home

Don't hold anyone on your knee, you better be
    true to me,
You better be true to me, you better be true
    to me.
Don't hold anyone on your knee, you're gettin'
    the third degree
When you come marchin' home

You're on your own where there is no phone,
And I can't keep tabs on you.
Be fair to me, I'll guarantee
This is one thing that I'll do
I won't sit under the apple tree with anyone else
    but you
'Til you come marchin' home.

Don't sit under the apple tree with anyone else
    but me.
I know the apple tree is reserved for you and me.
And I'll be true 'til you come marchin' home. ❖

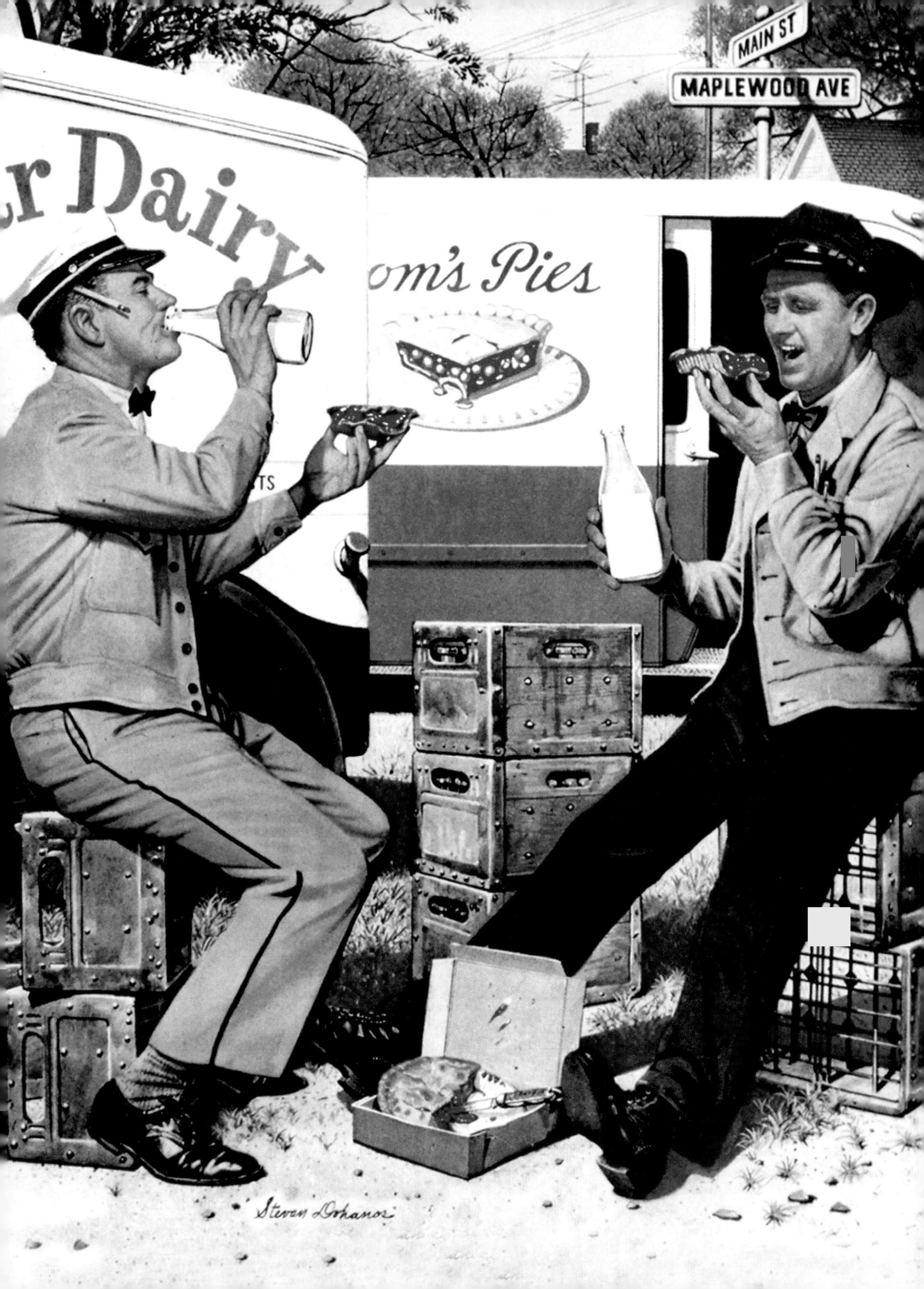
MAIN ST
MAPLEWOOD AVE
r Dairy
om's Pies
TS
Steven Dohanos

Back to Work

Chapter Two

When the Steven Dohanos painting on the facing page appeared on the cover of the *Saturday Evening Post* on Oct. 11, 1958, I couldn't help but think that it epitomized Working America during the boom years.

The milkman and the pieman, comrades in vans, are pictured exchanging and sharing the bounty of their individual jobs. Extrapolating a story from the painting, I figured that the men were good buddies from school who returned to their hometown after the war. One married his childhood sweetheart; the other, an English girl he met during the war. They landed delivery routes, but once a week met for an impromptu lunch, where they reminisced over a slab of Mom's Pies and a quart of milk from the Star Dairy.

To me, nearly 50 years after I first saw it, this slice of Americana caught on the artist's canvas still reflects the pride and satisfaction the drivers have in their jobs. That pride and satisfaction was common for so many of us back in the Good Old Days.

It seems today that some people think "work" is a four-letter word. Conversely, I think most of us were just glad to get back to work after the end of World War II.

The Great Depression had strangled the job market, and then the war had pulled almost all able-bodied young men out of the work force. The most essential male workers were exempt from military service, and Rosies of our land resolutely riveted or whatever else they needed to do to keep the war machine running and the home fires burning.

Now the boys were home, the economy was on the upswing and jobs—while not plenteous—were out there to be found. We were smart enough to know that it wasn't a return to the Roaring '20s, but we were still tempted to sing *Happy Days Are Here Again.*

I think those years of searching so desperately for a job made us so loyal and hardworking in the jobs we finally landed. Once it was relatively common for an employee to remain with the same company for 40 or 50 years—sometimes longer. That is as rare today as a professional athlete remaining with the same team throughout his career.

Like the milkman and the pieman, we were all relieved that the war years were over. And, like them, were we glad to be back to work again.

—*Ken Tate*

Shoe Trees to Christmas Trees

By Joe Curreri

To the soldiers who defend our freedom today, thanks for what you're doing. Thanks for who you are. Thanks for what you stand for. But after the war, after the exhilaration of coming home and being treated like a hero, you have important life decisions to make. You're young. Your life is ahead of you. Will you choose a career in the military? Will you adjust to civilian life? Will life be the same after the war? How will you cope? What will you do?

Those were the challenging questions I had to confront when I came home from World War II. Like millions of young men who had been drafted in the 1940s to fight for our freedom, we came home in 1945 after three years of brutal war. After horrific loss of life, with courage and conviction, deprivation and dedication, we defeated the villainous Nazi and Japanese empires.

On Sept. 7, 1945, after three years in the Army Air Force, I came home to my family and to an America whose flag waved high. It was the start of a booming era and a burgeoning economy. After years of blackouts and rationing, everyone felt that "happy days are here again."

As a civilian again, I had decisions to make. I could go to college under the GI Bill, as many others did. I could go back to my old job. But I did neither. I chose to go into business as my own boss.

I quickly learned that the storefront window is the key to the door. So I made a sign that read, "Owned and Operated by Veterans."

Our family included five boys. Two of my older brothers had opened a barber shop. Before the war, the younger brothers, including me, had worked for a big chain store, Ben Franklin Shoe Repair, which then had 15 stores in Philadelphia. When we three brothers came home after serving our country, we decided to open a shoe-repair shop as partners.

It was a perfect setup. Brothers Tony and Frank would do the actual shoe repair, and I was counterman and manager.

In January 1946, we opened a shop on Germantown Avenue, a busy commercial section including stores such as the Kresge 5 & 10, Sunray Drugs and the Linton Restaurant. A huge sign atop our store announced,

"Public Shoe Repair—While You Wait." Another sign in the window read, "Tony, Joe and Frank."

I quickly learned that the storefront window is the key to the door. So I made a sign that read, "Owned and Operated by Veterans," and turned the display window into a victory shrine displaying war items.

Most shoe-repair shops in those days were tiny, cluttered, dirty shops. Most of us remember from childhood the musty smells of leather and glue, and a man wearing an ink-stained apron greeting us.

"That will not be the case in *our* shop," I announced. We concluded that ours would be a large, 16- by 62-foot, modern, clean, enterprising store. The shoe-repair and machinery section would be partitioned off; comfortable booths would seat customers waiting for their shoes to be repaired. A large counter filled with shoe accessories would stand in the center. And I would wear a clean jacket and tie as I greeted customers with a smile.

To add a little humor, I composed, painted and posted signs in the shop: "You'll Never Reach Your Goal With A Hole In Your Sole"; "Shoemakers Never Die, They Stick To The Last"; and "Don't Be A Heel. Let Us Heal Your Sole."

With great fanfare, we opened to enthusiastic customers. Business was great. During World War II, everything had been rationed, so people had become accustomed to repairing rather than buying new.

Tony and Frank were expert shoe craftsmen. For my part, I became a congenial greeter, making a friend of each customer. I used my sales ability to advise them about the repairs they needed and I suggested products for taking care of their shoes. On prominent display were polishes, shoe dyes, shoe trees, insoles, pads, laces, shine kits and shine boxes. "Diversify and prosper," they say. We did.

In 1953 Holland was devastated by a flood, leaving their people in dire need of relief,

Upon entering the store, one was dazzled by the array of beautiful colors, lights and glitter. It created the maximum impulse to buy.

including shoes, blankets and clothing. That struck a sensitive chord with me. I had been shot down over Holland during the war, and when I bailed out, the Dutch Underground had helped me elude the Nazis and had saved my life.

So I reacted swiftly and posted a sign in our window: "We Are Collecting Shoes, Blankets and Clothing For Dutch Flood Victims. The Dutch Saved Many American Lives During The War. It's Our Turn Now."

People responded overwhelmingly. We collected two truckloads of clothing, shoes and blankets and sent them through the Dutch consulate to Holland. That outpouring of generosity renewed my faith in mankind. We got on TV for that.

But by 1956, a flood of less-expensive, foreign-import shoes was slowly eating away at the shoe-repair industry. Disposable shoes, and the kind that apparently never wear out—plastic and synthetic materials, and sneakers—encouraged a general exodus from the trade.

We decided that just being shoe repairmen wasn't enough. We had to become businessmen, merchandisers; more aggressive, more dedicated. We added more sales items to our store, such as carded items, novelties, cigars and cigarettes, candy and a Coke machine.

In November 1956, a man came into our shop and offered me "something I couldn't refuse." He offered to rent a small corner of our store and a little space in the window for one month. When he said he intended "to sell Christmas balls," I thought he was crazy. We agreed, provided he pay in advance.

When I saw the business he did, my brain started to whirl. Not only was he making spontaneous sales, but I noticed a new trade coming in. I grasped the potential immediately. After talking it over, we decided that this was a tremendous idea. I then set out to learn how. When that fellow came in with cases of stock, I noted the name of the wholesaler stamped on it.

The next year *I* bought the merchandise—

and we were in business. Each year I expanded, learning the how-to from the drugstores, 5 & 10s and supermarkets. It was a simple, inexpensive matter to rearrange the shop to handle the Christmas business. No elaborate fixtures were used. We just removed a few booths and added shelves, pegboards, and plywood on sawhorses.

Many of the people who came in couldn't believe that they were in a shoe-repair shop. That's when I enlightened them about our regular services. To help handle the increased traffic, I had my two boys, Joe and Frankie, come in after school. Later I added my wife, Irene.

Starting after Halloween, the window of our shop became a veritable fairyland of colorful lights, Christmas balls and ornaments that literally stopped shoppers in their tracks. Upon entering the store, one was dazzled by the array of beautiful colors, lights and glitter. It created the maximum impulse to buy.

People began looking for "the shoe-repair shop that sells Christmas balls." Typical signs and ads read: "Need laces? Polishes? Christmas balls?" and "From Shoe Trees to Christmas Trees." They drew laughs, but we three brothers had the last laugh—all the way to the bank. In two months, we had more customers in the store than the whole 10 previous months put together!

For 35 years we brothers prospered and

raised our families in the shoe-repair business. At the end, business began to fail. We closed the shop in 1981, after I had a heart attack. However, I did *not* retire. My two brothers have since gone to shoe-repair heaven, while I continue to write.

Today, shoe-repair shops are seldom seen. The soft *tap, tap, tap* of hammer on heels and the aromas of leather, polish and glue that used to waft from the shoemaker's open door on a warm spring day are vanishing. But when I do see a shoe-repair shop—or Christmas balls—it always brings back a treasure trove of memories, of the days when three brothers shared their hardships and their dreams. ❖

Operation Sound

By James T. Page

Getting back to work—and staying at work—after World War II wasn't always the easiest process for some of us in the Good Old Days.

I served on the *U.S.S. Nashville,* a light cruiser, during World War II. We spent most of our time in the Pacific and saw action in several sea battles and numerous bombardments. On one such occasion, we were ordered to the Solomon Islands to destroy the Munda Airfield and nearby barracks. This was a night operation and we were unaware of the exact time the firing was to begin.

I was standing on the main deck, behind the number three turret. All of a sudden, it fired a salvo (all three guns at once). I hurried for cover, but not before I was aware that the noise had affected my ears. I did not hear clearly for three days. I was ordered to report to the doctor, who told me it was only a temporary condition; my hearing would return to normal.

Time passed and when the war was over, I resigned from the Navy. My wife and I settled in Los Angeles. Our son, Tom, was born around the time I was attending the Los Angeles Police Academy. I graduated and became a police officer, and we bought a home in the San Fernando Valley. Soon our daughter was born. Everything was going great—I had a good profession and I was also taking night classes at the University of Southern California. We were a happy young family.

After I had been on the department for about four years, I noticed that I was having a problem hearing the police car radio. One day I had to testify in court and I couldn't understand the judge when he spoke to me. That same day I went to a hearing specialist who told me that my hearing was way off in both ears. Those turrets from long ago had left their mark. The doctor recommended a hearing aid.

In the golden days of the 1950s, hearing aids were not the innocuous things they are today. They were about the size of a pack of cigarettes. You had to carry it in your pocket, and a very visible wire ran from it to your ear.

No way was I going to wear one of those things! I didn't think the public would have much confidence in a police officer with a wire coming out of his ear. Nor was I sure that the department would even allow me to wear one on duty. I saw my career going down the tubes.

Then we had some friends over one Sunday afternoon and, fortunately, one of them worked at the Veterans Administration's Sawtelle Hospital. Our friend told me that there was a doctor there who did operations to help people with hearing problems. Our friend recommended that I go see him, and I did. I soon learned that Dr. Mumma was one of two doctors that performed a new operation called a "fenestration." The procedure involved removing the inner eardrum and replacing it with a piece of skin from the thigh.

Dr. Mumma was a remarkable person as well as an outstanding surgeon. My operation was so successful that he operated on the other ear with equal results. My career was saved and I stayed with the department for 30 years, finally retiring as a lieutenant. The sounds I hear now are no longer the raging blasts of so long ago, but the sweet sound of Josephine, my wife of almost 61 years, saying, "Good night. I love you." ❖

No way was I going to wear one of those things! I didn't think the public would have much confidence in a police officer with a wire coming out of his ear.

I Even Go Texas!

By Charles C. Walther

Shortly after being discharged from the U.S. Army in 1947, I went back to work as a door-to-door vacuum cleaner salesman. The company office was located in Waukegan, Ill. In the process of selling the product, I contacted many residents in that fine city and surrounding communities. My compensation was straight commission, so if I didn't sell, I didn't earn.

I rang many doorbells, knocked on many doors and made product presentations to many people. The people I met were typical honest, hardworking, Midwestern citizens. It was an excellent learning experience, and I learned a great deal about my fellow Americans.

Though it happened more than 50 years ago, there is one special experience that I still remember vividly. It made me appreciate our wonderful opportunities in America more than all the history books I have ever read or political speeches I have ever heard.

Experience had taught me that people who lived in upstairs apartments were least likely to be visited by salesmen and were therefore excellent prospects.

The sun was setting late on a summer evening. Although I had made several sales that day, I was following my employer's suggestion: Whenever you are ready to quit, you should make at least one more call. Accordingly, I lugged my demonstration machine and equipment up the back stairs of a two-story, somewhat dilapidated building. Experience had taught me that people who lived in upstairs apartments were the least likely to be visited by salesmen and were therefore excellent prospects.

I knocked on the door of the second-floor apartment. A friendly gentleman who was older than I was opened the door and said "Hello" in broken English. As he invited me in, I realized from his speech that he was not a native-born American.

We went into the parlor and he suggested that I sit in an overstuffed chair that was probably always saved for guests. He wanted to talk with me. His wife was very gracious and offered me a cold drink and cookies. She served the drink from a large ornate pitcher—obviously a family heirloom that they had brought to America.

As it turned out, he and his wife had lived in America for just a short time. They had emigrated from one of the Balkan countries shortly after World War II ended. They were both employed by a local pharmaceutical company in neighboring North Chicago, Ill.

The man was very animated and talkative. He talked about many things. We communicated by using gestures, his broken English and the smattering of German we both knew. Finally he shared what he considered to be a most humorous and wonderful experience.

After they had lived in Waukegan for several months, he and his wife learned that some of their friends and former countrymen had also come to America, and had settled in Milwaukee, Wis. After contacting these friends, they decided it would be nice to visit them. My new American friend described what happened next:

"One day after work, I put on suit and go to police station. I stand by front desk and wait for officer. He not notice me since working on papers. Finally, officer look up and ask me what I want. I tell him I want to go Milwaukee and see friends.

"He say, 'What the heck do you want me to do, drive you there? Just go.'

"I say, 'Please sir, I need permit since Milwaukee is in state of Wisconsin.'

"He said, 'What is this, joke or something?'

"I explain that where I used to live, you always need permission from police to go from one area to another.

"He laugh. Finally he stop laughing and said, 'Look, now you are in the United States and you can go anywhere you want unless you break the law. Just don't speed and don't drink if you drive.'

"I was very happy, so I shake his hand and say 'Thank you, sir, and goodbye.' I was so happy when I leave that I almost cry."

My new friend then stood in the middle of his parlor, and using gestures and very emotional, animated speech, he said, "In America I go where I want, go Washington, go California—I even go Texas and not need permit! I love America!"

I didn't sell a vacuum cleaner at that house, but after that demonstration of love for my coun-try, my heart was filled with pride. As I went back down the stairs, my eyes filled with tears. I looked skyward and silently said, "Thank you, Lord, for blessing us in America." ❖

Some serious posters—and some humorous ones—were produced, featuring this strong, competent woman. She appeared dressed in overalls or corduroy pants, in leather boots and bandanas.

Rosie the Riveter

By Ross Princiotto

During World War II, women in the United States were known as "the third force" and "girls without guns." Many of them abandoned their chores on the home front and went to work in the factories while the men 18–39 years of age fought in the war.

When war was declared, the Army, Navy and Marine Corps were mobilized immediately. More than 16 million GIs left to serve in the Armed Forces. In their absence, women stepped in to take up duties men once had held. Their benefits were great; they earned stipends from soldiers' wages, paychecks of their own, and camaraderie with both female and male companions. In the process, women gained self-reliance.

This turnabout in the workforce completely changed the role of women in our country. The symbol of these women who loved, served and supported their country became known as "Rosie the Riveter."

Some serious posters—and some humorous ones—were produced, featuring this strong, competent woman. She appeared dressed in overalls or corduroy pants, in leather boots and bandanas. During those war years, most women's clothing was made of rayon and inexpensive fabrics; other products, such as cotton and wool, were precious, and reserved for the defense industry. The GIs were always awarded the best!

Did the women complain about the gritty conditions in the factories? No, they did not. In fact, they enjoyed the opportunity to help the war effort, and their ability to endure the hardships in their new, unusual roles pleased them.

A new era for women had begun. They were thrilled to be out in this "new world." Many women believed that participating in the workforce was patriotic, and it was one of the highlights of their young lives. These "girls without guns" even insisted that they had fun during the war era.

Women excelled in fulfilling their obligations to their country. They were accepted in the man's world as riveters, welders, inspectors, laborers, crane operators and even truck drivers. In the process, they learned and produced much better than their male bosses ever would have believed.

With the end of World War II, the jobs that had been created for the defense effort disappeared. Men returned to take their old jobs, if they wanted them, or to search for newer, more lucrative positions. In the aftermath, many women were content to return to their domestic duties, nurturing families and having children who would become the "baby boomers." Others, however, complained when veterans forced sisters, wives and daughters to return to household responsibilities.

With that experience in the wartime workforce behind them, many former "Rosies" went on to work in a plethora of careers, including management positions. And thus one-time homemakers found themselves doing work they never would have imagined otherwise. And they loved it!

Yes, the days of Rosie the Riveter are fondly remembered by many former "Rosies," including Jennette Huttrail, a wartime crane operator. "See that crane, way, way up there?" she declared to her grandchildren as she pointed skyward. "Grandma used to run a crane like that during the Second World War!"

Her grandchildren smiled while Jennette stood proud yet misty-eyed. ❖

Thanksgiving at Christmas

By Leta Fulmer Harvey

*S*aturday afternoon, Dec. 20, 1952

My busy fingers kept time to the beat of *Jingle Bells* as the radio filled Keller's Fur Company with the sounds of Christmas. I finished the last cross-stitch on the Keller label, tacking it into place. With a pat of satisfaction, I cushioned the mink stole with tissue paper and carefully folded it into a bright red box. One more coat was finished for the approaching holiday season.

The music ended abruptly with a news flash: "There's been a break in the gas line near Leaven-worth, Kansas. This is the source of St. Joseph's sup-ply. Hopefully, it will be repaired in a short time. And now—on with the music."

The words had little impact on us as we rushed from task to task. This was our busy sea-son. Nothing quite filled the bill for a Christmas present like a gift of fur. We laughed and chatted and drank coffee while we stitched last minute take-ups on recently purchased items. We'd almost forgotten the news bulletin when the announcer broke in again.

"Sorry, folks, to interrupt again, but this situation has grown increasingly serious. The break has been found 10 feet underground, near the town of Beverly. They're calling out extra help. But that big gas tank at Fourth and Cedar is beginning to shrink like a leaky balloon. It's almost a certainty that within the hour, our gas supply will be gone. The gas company has issued this warning. I repeat—this is a warning: 'When the gas is gone, be sure to turn off all gas jets and pilot lights. This is vital to prevent explosions.' We'll keep you informed. Now, back to our program."

Music burst forth again. But our festive mood had changed to one of concern. Almost unbe-lieving, we turned to stare at each other. Though Keller's was steam-heated, most of us were utterly dependent on gas at home. It still seemed unreal, difficult to take the threat seriously.

A friend turned to me with a laugh. "Oh well, the whole bunch of you can go out in the country with me. I've got bottled gas, you know." We teased her a bit about her home bulging at the seams with a big group of fur workers. But her encouraging words turned out to be more prophetic than jovial.

"Thank goodness it's not zero weather," I remarked as I got into the car where my husband waited. "I suppose you've heard about the gas?"

"Thank goodness it's not zero weather," I remarked as I got into the car where my husband waited. "I suppose you've heard about the gas?"

"I've more than heard about it," Jimmie grunted. "Everything's turned off at home. The gas fizzled out some time ago."

"Well," I said, struggling for optimism, "sure-ly we can stand it until the gas comes back on. Since they're working on it, it can't be too long."

The rooms at home were already cooling off. Six-year-old Rosemary peeked out from the cocoonlike warmth of a wooly blanket in which she was snuggled on the couch. Eleven-year-old Johnnie wore a heavy jacket while waiting for his favorite between-meal snack to emerge from the pop-up toaster. Leaving my coat on, I rummaged around for the one-burner hot plate. But even before our scanty meal of hot soup and sandwiches was finished, the chill was beginning to creep into our bones. How could a house cool off so fast?

"Say," Jimmie said, heading for the basement, "that little, round kerosene stove is old, but I think it still works. Maybe it will help."

Well, it did a little, as we surrounded it with our shivering bodies. But its rusted innards soon put out a cloud of smoke, and the air fairly reeked with throat-burning fumes.

We listened to the news as it was repeated, enlarged upon. Everyone was urged to find a warm place to wait out the emergency. At the very best, it would be several hours before heat could be restored. Central, Benton and Lafayette High Schools, all steam heated, were being opened to the public. The National Guard was moving in cots. All hospitals, including the State Hospital, had standby heat, and patients from many nursing homes were being transferred to those buildings.

Although the break had been mended four hours after it had been located, it was an overwhelming task to check the more than 20,000 homes and businesses to be sure that all gas was turned off before service could be restored. I stared at my shivering family. I could almost feel the comfort of the shop at Keller's. My employers had insisted that we were all welcome to return and stay as long as necessary.

"Come on," I decided. "We're not going to stay here and freeze. Everybody will be down with colds. Start gathering up food and stuff and we'll head back to work."

Jimmie and I raided the icebox and cookie jar. Rosemary came up with several boxes of cherry chocolates (meant for Christmas) and Johnnie searched frantically through his stacks of comic books, looking for the most current issues. We turned off the oil burner, checked to see that all the gas was off, locked the house and left.

Several others had arrived at the shop before us. Coffee perked in the big pot. We sighed with relief when the steam heat gradually thawed our cold bodies and we could wriggle out of our coats. Everyone had brought groceries of some sort. The pop machine served as an emergency ice chest for our perishables. And the little two-burner hot plate was kept glowing.

The radio kept us in touch with the outside world, describing the confusion and problems that were suddenly plaguing our town. Firemen were busy extinguishing fires from overheated stoves and fireplaces. Mayor Dale, declaring an emergency, had alerted a defense corps of 2,500. Walnut Log Company was offering wood to anyone who would come and get it. Enterprise Furniture Company had sold out of oil and electric heaters. Two additional truckloads had sold out in two hours. Luckily for all of us, the light and power company had immediately converted to other fuel. Kissing cousins suddenly became close relatives—if they had a fireplace, or burned oil or propane. Hotels with any kind of heat were swamped with customers. Most restaurants were closed. In fact, most of our town was utterly dependent on gas. It was our common denominator—and it was gone!

Saturday night, Dec. 20
It was nearing midnight. The streetlights were reflected in the snow-covered streets. I stood in the Thrift Shop doorway and watched the activity at the gas company across the street. We all

1952 White Sewing Machine ad, House of White Birches nostalgia archives held on tightly to the hope that the temperature would drop no farther than the present 18 degrees. Frozen water pipes would indeed add insult to injury.

Hours before, the kids had been bedded down in the fitting rooms. They slept there on sofas, cuddled in the luxurious warmth of new fur coats. Jimmie dozed in a big chair—he could sleep anywhere.

About a dozen of us stayed up that first night, each doing exactly as he pleased. We were a close-knit group, having worked together for so many years. Completely at ease with each other, some chose to sit in silence. Others kept up animated conversations. A few just wandered about disconsolately, constantly misplacing cups of lukewarm coffee or half-eaten doughnuts. And always there was the incessant voice of the radio, presenting up-to-the minute reports on the situation.

At long last, utter weariness overcame my curiosity and concern. Checking once more on the kids, I prepared a makeshift bed of secondhand coats. Under and over me, they gave off an aura of moth crystals and unclean fur. But they were warm and comforting as I snuggled down to sleep.

Sunday morning, Dec. 21

I awoke to the sound of the familiar chatter on the radio. The aroma of perking coffee yanked me from my furry bed. Dousing my face with cold water, I hurried to join the group. Someone had made a quick trip home, returning with a toaster and a jar of jelly, the morning paper and a jigsaw puzzle.

The *News-Press* had converted to other fuel and had managed to get out the Sunday edition. Black headlines streaked across its face: "Break Leaves City Without Gas." We'd already heard most of the details on the radio, but reading the paper put it before us in black and white.

The hours seemed to drag. Johnnie eagerly ran errands for everyone, anxious for activity of any sort. Rosemary scrubbed our coffee cups until they shone like new. Finally she dusted and sorted fancy buttons that would eventually adorn fur coats—anything to make the time pass! Jimmie napped, wandered in and out. Cards were available for anyone who wanted to play, but concentration was a problem. The jigsaw puzzle

was set up on the nailing table; occasionally a passerby would fit one more crooked piece into the unfinished picture.

Most of the men made hasty trips home to check on icy houses. They brought back additional food, clothing and reading material.

The radio continued to blare out its urgent warnings. "Be sure that all gas is turned off. Service cannot be restored until a house-by-house check is completed." The phones in the shop were kept busy as we checked on friends and relatives. More or less isolated in my warm little haven of security, I listened with interest as a friend filled me in on her situation.

"Well," she laughed, "you should see us here. Out went our big gas stove and this old potbellied antique moved in again. Even had to cut a hole in my new wallpaper for the big stovepipe! But we're doing fine. Half the neighbors have moved in, all bringing food. You'd be surprised how well I manage to cook on the top of this old relic! We have either a pot of soup beans or vegetable stew simmering all the time—coffee, too. The grown-ups head for home at night, but the kids stay here. We've put all the mattresses side-by-side in this warm room, and I watch over them like an old mother hen."

We found the situation was similar everywhere, as people pooled their heat and food to share with each other. It was a community project that really went over the top, and without any ballyhoo. Everyone just seemed to do what came naturally. Many people who'd gone away left their houses unlocked so they could be checked. Even so, accounts of vandalism and theft were rare. In this emergency, there was one central theme: Get the gas back on.

And gas was coming in. The big tank was ballooning again. But we had to wait. Feeling scroungy, disheveled and bored to death, I listened to the news, paced the floor and drank endless cups of coffee.

Finally it was nighttime again. Once more I peered toward the gas company where weary men trudged in and out. And I felt a sudden sting of guilt for my selfish impatience. After all, I was warm and well-fed. And certainly anything but overworked. These tired men were working frantically.

The group in the fur shop wandered in and out. Some found other roosting places for that second night. We stayed put. Another night slid by with all of us bedded down in every variety of fur, from mink to rabbit.

Monday, Dec. 22

A workday! It was a relief to have something to busy my idle hands. All day we stitched and pressed, inspected and fitted without interruption. Our customers evidently were content to hibernate; they'd do their shopping another day.

Time crawled by, enlivened only by the encouraging news on the radio. Workmen were canvassing the town from top to bottom. Civil Defense, Red Cross, light company, gas company, police and fire departments, plumbers and electricians—side by side, all qualified personnel worked feverishly to return our town to normalcy. Slowly, very slowly, service was being restored. The first houses received gas at about 1 o'clock Monday afternoon.

It was almost quitting time when my boss appeared in the doorway. "Hey, Leta, you're wanted on the phone."

"I've got the heat on!" Jimmie sounded relieved. "Everything's all right, but this house is still like a deepfreeze. Better stay there awhile. Soon as it warms up a bit, I'll come after you and the kids."

Ah, home at last! Everything was just as we'd left it. The Christmas tree stood there, waiting, with its burden of colored lights and glittering tinsel. But our small house was far from warm. Everything we touched brought on a rash of goose pimples!

When the heat finally began to work its magic, I slipped out of my coat and breathed a sigh of thanksgiving at Christmastime. Still uneasy, I awoke at midnight to the sound of sleet beating an icy tattoo on the roof. When I awoke again the next morning, I discovered than an additional 3½ inches of snow had fallen.

More than ever, I was thankful to be in my own home—and warm!

The emergency was almost over. Although gas had been returned to our city on Monday after a lapse of 45 hours, many homes were still without heat well into Tuesday. Needless to say, there were accidents—personal injuries and property damage. But in proportion to the area involved, the percentage was very small. Without the cooperation and careful supervision of those men who had worked so hard, it might very easily have been a disaster area.

Each time I pass that big gas tank at Fourth and Cedar, I remember how it once squished down to almost nothing. Oh yes, it's still there. But with the passing years, it has outlived its original purpose. With the increased number of customers, it would hold only about an hour's supply of gas today. Now it is used for grain storage. Today, our gas reaches us through multiple lines; it would be nearly impossible for that type of emergency to confront us again.

As I wrote this article, I asked my family what memories stood out most vividly in their minds. Many years later, Rosemary remembered that for the first time, she had more cherry chocolates than she could eat. Johnnie remembered the bouncy comfort of a fur-coat bed and the sleek feel of the satin linings. Jimmie, the practical one, recalled shivering visits to an icy house, and battles with balky gas jets and pilot lights.

Even after all these years, my own memories still shine crystal bright in retrospect: the sight of the gas company beyond the Thrift Shop door; the comforting knowledge that my family was safe and warm, within the call of my voice; the cheerful perk of the never-empty coffeepot; the unceasing voice of the radio; the jigsaw puzzle that never saw completion; and old friends who made dreary days shine with laughter and foolishness.

That's the energy crisis I remember—three unforgettable days just before Christmas in 1952. ❖

Those Wonderful Trains

By Lucille Armstrong Anton

In 1945 I started working at the Great Northern Railway offices at Jackson and Fourth streets, St. Paul, Minn. I could hardly wait for vacation! One of the perks of working for the Great Northern was being eligible to get free passes to ride the trains.

Before World War II ended in 1945, the trains had been crowded with servicemen. Travel by rail—or any other way, for that matter—was only undertaken as a matter of necessity. But after the war, we didn't have to sit on suitcases in the aisle anymore (although that hadn't been exactly boring).

I was living in a rooming house. With no responsibilities, I was footloose, fancy free and ready for new adventures. I took several trips during the years that I worked in the Great Northern freight receipts office. In 1946, a co-worker, Mary, went with me to Seattle on the *Empire Builder*. At Seattle we boarded the *S.S. Princess Alice* for a five-hour trip on Puget Sound to Victoria, British Columbia. I had never seen mountains or the ocean until I got my job at the railroad office, and the marvelous scenery thrilled me.

> *Our ride on the train was not totally free; we paid for our berths in the Pullman car on the Empire Builder, and our meals in the dining car.*

Lunch cost $1 at the Empress Hotel, which was owned and operated by the Canadian Pacific Railway. Our bus tour took us past the British Columbia Provincial Parliament buildings. They were huge and ornate. Besides the large dome in the center, several smaller domes topped the corners and middle section. It was the most magnificent "castle" we'd ever seen.

We went to the Butchart Gardens. I remember the uniqueness of the sunken garden, the Japanese garden, the Italian garden and the rose garden. Then we returned to Seattle on the *S.S. Princess Victoria*. We took a bus tour of Seattle. The Pontoon Bridge on Lake Washington fascinated us.

The next year, I accompanied two co-workers, Rita and Marion, to Glacier National Park. We had paid for our weeklong tour of Glacier, for the sightseeing buses and for our lodging at the park hotels before leaving St. Paul. Our ride on the train was not totally free; we paid for our berths in the Pullman car on the *Empire Builder*, and our meals in the dining car. The first dinner was $2.75 and the second, $1.25. The tables had white linen napkins and tablecloths and the waiters looked spiffy in their white jackets.

September 1948 Railroad Magazine, House of White Birches nostalgia archives

At Glacier we stayed at the Glacier Park Hotel, Many Glacier Hotel and the Prince of Wales Hotel in neighboring Waterton Lakes Park in Canada. As our sightseeing bus traveled on the Going-to-the-Sun Highway, the spectacular scenery impressed us. Our gear-jammer (bus driver) pulled into a lookout area at Logan Pass so we could get out for a few minutes. We made snowballs—in July. The gear-jammers were college students, working there for the summer.

When we got into Canada at Waterton Lakes Park, the mountains were even more majestic. One night while we were staying at the Prince of Wales Hotel, we experienced an electrical storm. The thunder boomed and echoed between the huge mountains; it was the loudest thunder we'd ever heard.

Launches took us on rides on Waterton Lake at the Prince of Wales Hotel; on Swift Current Lake at the Many Glacier Hotel; and on Lake McDonald at the Lake McDonald Hotel.

My next vacation gave me a chance to go to Winnipeg on a pass with another friend. Then we spent a week on the *S.S. Keenora*, a freighter that took about 100 passengers each week on

Author Lucille Armstrong Anton stepping on the train and giving her last good-byes.

Lake Winnipeg. At that time, the Cree Indian settlements around the lake relied on the boat to bring them supplies. While the crew unloaded sacks of flour, salt, sugar and other stuff, we could walk around the settlements until we heard the boat whistle, which meant we had five minutes to get back on board. The meals on the *S.S. Keenora* made each of us gain about five pounds during that one week.

Yes, I did work the other 51 weeks of the year. I was a comptometer operator in those days. That machine is now obsolete, but it could add, subtract, multiply and divide. It was the calculating machine long before computers. In our department, we figured the cost of shipping iron ore and coal by the amount per ton.

I miss those wonderful trains nowadays. That era was special because we could go almost anywhere on the railroad. Besides my vacation trips, I took many weekend trips to see my folks in Wisconsin, and an overnight on the train brought us to Chicago. Sometimes, after riding the train home from Chicago on Sunday night, we'd go right to work after rolling into the Union Station in St. Paul. It took awhile to catch up on sleep, though. ❖

Dinner for Mattie

By Glen Herndon

*I*n our community of Modesto, Calif., the Good Old Days just after World War II brought a revival of the popular Aluminum Cookware Dinners.

With the war behind us, aluminum once again could be turned to civilian needs. Long-time makers of the leading line of cookware—and several arch rivals—sent sales representatives to people's homes, where they cooked a complete dinner while making a well-choreographed sales presentation. All sorts of premiums and other incentives were offered. Those dinners were mighty easy to book, for there was a great pent-up demand.

The year 1946 was a happy one, when we could get things again.

My older brother, Herbert, lately a captain in the Army Air Corps Supply, needed money to revive his home contracting business. Before the war, he and his twin, Herman, had been home builders and general contractors. Now, both would have to work at whatever they could get for a while to "get on their feet."

Good-looking, ebullient, and blessed with a beautiful young wife, Hallie, who was a gourmet cook, Herbert immediately shot to the top spot in sales. Herbert and Hallie recruited me, then in junior college, to go along as their "right-hand man." Of course, it was more for scullery duty than anything else. We always left the host's kitchen spotless.

I did have another qualification, though: At age 18, I was an adequate cook. For many years I had stood at Mother's elbow in the kitchen,

Well, of course, she had whispered in my ear that she knew the high quality of our brand; after all, it had been on the market, except during the war, for more than 50 years!

watching everything she did. So even though I was only 12 when she died near the beginning of the war, I could fend for myself in the kitchen. Dad and I "batched it," and he bought me a cookbook, which taught me many other things.

My sister-in-law, Hallie, trained me in all aspects of the prescribed cookware dinner. Sometimes she left me to the kitchen preparations while she joined Herbert for the living-room presentation.

I never expected it, but one day, Herbert announced that he had booked a dinner at Mattie Streeter's home. "She is the chief cook at the high school cafeteria, and she tells me they prepare and serve about 1,600 meals a day, most things 'from scratch,'" Herbert said. "Boy, if I can sell her, we'll get lots of referrals! You know her?"

"Oh, yes!" I replied. Mattie was one of the nicest people I knew at the high school. "And you know how Mother taught us to show respect for our elders? Well, she wouldn't hear of my calling her 'Mrs. Streeter.' No, sir! None of that! 'I'm just plain old Mattie to you. But now you clean up your plate; I'll be checking that you do!'" And off she'd go to "mother" someone else.

The very prospect of going to Mattie's home, and preparing a meal for her and her family in her very own kitchen—now *that* was daunting. I knew her well enough to know that if she didn't like what she heard or tasted, she'd say so. Big Brother didn't seem the least bit worried—but then he was always confident!

Then, at the last minute, disaster struck! Hallie was bedridden with the flu. But Herbert had a tight schedule; Mattie had her own plans; the dinner must go forward or be postponed indefinitely! Of all his bookings, Herbert felt Mattie's was the most important to him, and so he said, "Well, there's nothing for it but for you and me to put on the dinner at Mattie's. Think you can handle it?"

Had it been anyone other than Mattie, I would have been boldly confident. But though I tried not to show my lack of confidence, I must have because Herbert said, "Now get a grip on yourself! We can do this!"

When we got to Mattie's that night, she had what seemed like a houseful of hungry people, and she came out to see what was going on in her kitchen. The first thing she did was give me a big bear hug, and then she whispered something in my ear. Then she commanded, "But don't tell your brother!"

After that, I calmed down and followed all the prescribed steps I'd helped Hallie with so often. All our demonstrations and the roast beef dinner were well received. I have never forgotten that evening because Mattie said, "I can't tell you how I enjoyed this! I didn't have to cook!"

After the meal, I went about my scullery duties, hearing my brother's sales pitch off in the distance. Just as I was finishing up, he came through the door with a beaming Mattie.

"I'm buying your largest set!" Mattie announced. And with a wink, she said, "This handsome brother of yours is some salesman. I think he could sell snowballs to the Eskimos!"

Then she said to Herbert, "How I've longed for this day! It will be so nice to replace my old, worn-out utensils."

Well, of course, she had whispered in my ear that she knew the high quality of our brand; after all, it had been on the market, except during the war, for more than 50 years! "You just relax," she had told me. "I'm sure our meal will be fit for a king!"

We both walked out of there that night with light hearts. She'd recognized Herbert for the crackerjack salesman he was, and as for me, she seemed to think I was a pretty good chef. ❖

1957 Kitchen Craft ad, House of White Birches nostalgia archives

The Best Advice

By Jack Friedberg

When World War II ended in September 1945, and I came back to the United States, the first thing the Army did was send me home for more than a week, still in uniform, to use up my unspent leaves. I hadn't had a leave the entire time I was overseas.

I decided to use that time for two purposes. First, I set out to become reacquainted with my daughter, who had been a 3-week-old infant when I left and who was now a walking, talking, laughing, crying little lady going on 2.

My first night home was heartbreaking. I was helping my wife put her to bed when my wife said, "Kiss Daddy goodnight." I opened my arms, but she turned away from me and blew a kiss to my picture, in Army uniform, that stood on the dresser. That was the only "Daddy" she had known until then.

But that problem was soon solved. The picture was relegated to a dresser drawer and she learned that a warm kiss and hug from a real-life Daddy were far superior to a blown kiss.

We also established another bond. The first time she fell down and got a boo-boo, I dug up my Purple Heart medal and pinned it on her dress. She stopped crying and proudly showed Mommy her medal. Mommy gave her a big kiss and praised her for her bravery.

We kept that up—even when I knew she was faking it—until the Purple Heart got lost, but I didn't care. Between the extra discharge points and making my daughter happy, I got my money's worth out of that medal.

Later, I found that I could anticipate what the foreman would do and I began to make my own suggestions. He saw what I was doing and encouraged me.

My second objective was to check out the job market. The points needed for discharge were dropping rapidly. I figured it would only be a week or two before I came back home as a civilian. (Actually, it was only four days.) I wanted to be ready to go back to work, but I had decided to change careers, and this was my best chance to do so.

Before I had gone into the Army, I had been a printer, but I had become dissatisfied with setting type to fit other people's layouts. I wanted to do more creative work, and make layouts for other printers to follow. I had been taking a course in advertising layout, which had been interrupted by my military service.

First I decided to go back and consult with my old layout teacher, who gave me the best advice I ever received: "Don't throw away your knowledge of type and printing." He advised, "Check out the advertising typographers first. Besides," and this clinched the argument, "typographers make more money than layout artists."

For those not familiar with the difference, a typographer is to a printer what a specialist is to a general practitioner. A printer might have 40 or 50 typefaces in his shop, while a typographer has 200 or 300, and he chooses among them as carefully as an artist chooses his colors.

I made the rounds of advertising typographers, notifying them that I was not available right away, but would be in a couple of weeks. There wasn't much need for layout artists—the advertising agencies supplied their own layouts. But one foreman asked me if I could do markup. Markup means figuring the size of type needed to fit the space allotted in the layout. I had done some of that as a printer, and I was pretty accurate, so I jumped at the chance.

I reported for work the following Monday. Instead of a blue work shirt, open at the collar, I wore a shirt and tie. Instead of a shop, I worked in an office. I didn't have to wear a printer's apron to keep my clothes clean; they didn't get dirty, which my wife appreciated.

It only took me two weeks to realize that there wasn't enough markup to keep me busy full time. I didn't know how long the company would be willing to pay me for 40 hours' work when I only worked about 15 hours per week, so I decided to take advantage of another skill from my printing days. I shared the office with the proofreader, and he was often behind in his work. First, I checked with him to make sure he didn't think I was invading his territory.

Typographer setting type. Photo by Donald Uhrbrock Circa 1962. Time Life Pictures/Getty Images

The proofreader was pleased by my offer, so I told the foreman that I wanted to fill my idle time by helping the proofreader. He agreed, and I was soon working full time.

I was amazed at the foreman's visual skill. When I took an ad to him after proofreading it, he would instruct the typesetter to "Move the headline up six points and set the subhead one size larger," and an ad that was only ordinary would suddenly spring to life!

Later, I found that I could anticipate what the foreman would do and I began to make my own suggestions. He saw what I was doing and encouraged me.

Things went along smoothly for two more years until one day, the owner, the last surviving partner, walked into the shop with his two sons and announced that they were taking over the business. Neither of them was a typographer.

The foreman quit immediately! He had been promised the business when the old man retired, and now he had been double-crossed. I assumed I was next in line for the job since I had been doing similar work to the foreman's, but the sons had different ideas. One of them declared himself foreman. I soon wound up doing his thinking for him—and when I complained, I was offered a 5-cent-an-hour raise!

In the meantime, I heard that the former foreman was negotiating to buy a business. I told him I wanted to work for him. He made me a counteroffer. He was having trouble raising the money, so if I could get some money together, he wanted me as a partner. To make a long story short, we went into business together.

Starting up a new business was rough, and we worked many 60- and 70-hour weeks, but eventually it paid off. We started with 14 employees, and when we sold out and retired many years later, we had 43 employees, including a lot of our old colleagues whom we hired when our old shop folded because of incompetent management.

My old layout teacher is long gone, but I like to think he is looking down from somewhere, pleased that he was able to have such a profound effect on me and my family. ❖

Home to a New Life

By O.C. Westerfield

World War II created a new world. Millions of men in the cities discovered that there was life beyond the cities and towns they knew. I was a Depression kid, raised in a rural setting in Arkansas. I had never been away from home before the war. Who knew there was so much out there?

I decided that after the war, I would never raise another crop of cotton. After considering everything, I decided I wanted to be an electrician. I could get money from the GI Bill while going to school.

The economy was in a bad state. After quite a bit of looking, I found a place where I could work as an electrician's apprentice. I would not receive any pay, however, until the economy picked up. My service officer agreed, so I went to work for nothing, but received $90 a month from the government.

Pepsi ad, 1960 Boys' Life Magazine, House of White Birches nostalgia archives

I was a married man with a child, so we looked for a house. But houses were next to impossible to find. We finally found and rented a one-room apartment.

After a bit, I began to receive 50 cents an hour at work. That 50 cents an hour along with $90 a month from Uncle Sam seemed like a fortune to me.

Eventually I decided I was not getting enough education, so I went to the Coyne Trade School in Chicago. I had to leave my family for a while, but I was able to send them money and go to school. I attended classes from 6 a.m.–3 p.m., then went to work at 4 p.m. at a part-time job in the post office, where I worked until 11 p.m. This was quite a change for a farm boy.

When I finished at the Coyne School, I returned to my old job in Arkansas for $1 an hour. Through the GI Bill, I still received $90 a month from the government for a short time. In my opinion, the GI Bill of Rights was the best thing that ever happened to the returning soldier.

Back at my old electrician job, I had to leave my name at the dispatch office, as I was the only one who made service calls at night. I felt like a doctor.

At that time, a Pepsi-Cola plant was opening in our little town, and I was given the job of installing all the machinery. After I got it installed, the owner offered me the job of production manager, and I grabbed it. After several years, I relocated to South Bend, Ind., and earned more money for running a soft-drink plant there. At one time or another, I ran plants all over the United States.

I think that's pretty darn good for a country boy from the hills of Arkansas with a fifth-grade education. I did this and raised a family of three boys and a girl just by taking advantage of the opportunities available to me in this great country. And two of my sons followed me into the soft-drink business. ❖

Work Songs

*L*egend has it that a newspaper reporter was responsible for dubbing the little steam train that puffed out of Chattanooga, Tenn., as the "Chattanooga Choo Choo."

Lyricist Mack Gordon was inspired to tap out a set of lyric words featuring the name of the little engine, and *Chattanooga Choo Choo* became one of those songs that kept us tapping our toes as we headed back to work in the Good Old Days.

The song, with music by Harry Warren, was introduced by Glenn Miller and his orchestra in 1941 and was featured in the movie *Sun Valley Serenade*. The little steam locomotive kept its rhythmic beat throughout World War II and beyond. Today, after over 60 years, it continues as a favorite for working men and women everywhere.

Chattanooga Choo Choo
Pardon me, boy,
Is that the Chattanooga Choo Choo?
Track twenty-nine,
Boy, you can gimme a shine.
I can afford
To board a Chattanooga Choo Choo.
I've got my fare
And just a trifle to spare.

You leave the Pennsylvania Station
'Bout a quarter to four.
Read a magazine and then
You're in Baltimore.
Dinner in the diner,
Nothing could be finer,
Than to have your
Ham an' eggs in Carolina.

When you hear the whistle blowin'
Eight to the bar
Then you know that Tennessee
Is not very far.
Shovel all the coal in
Gotta keep it rollin'
Woo, woo, Chattanooga there you are
There's gonna be

A certain party at the station.
Satin and lace
I used to call "funny face."
She's gonna cry
Until I tell her that I'll never roam.
So Chattanooga Choo Choo
Won't you choo-choo me home?
Chattanooga Choo Choo
Won't you choo-choo me home?

Sometimes the grind of the workweek weighed heavy upon us, and once in a while we longed for the days when our back-to-work life wouldn't be quite so frenetic.

Maybe that is what Hoagy Carmichael had in mind when he wrote the words and music to *Up a Lazy River* in 1931. It continued in popularity through the war and into the boom years. The Mills Brothers recorded one of the better-known renditions in 1967.

Up a Lazy River
Up a lazy river by the old millstream.
That lazy, hazy river where we both can dream.
Linger in the shade of an old oak tree.
Throw away your troubles, dream a dream with me.

Up a lazy river where the robin's song
Wakes up in the mornin', as we roll along.
Blue skies up above; everyone's in love.
Up a lazy river, how happy we will be, now,
Up a lazy river with me.

Up a lazy river by the old mill run.
That lazy, lazy river in the noon day sun.
You can linger in the shade of that fine ole tree
Throw, away your troubles, baby, dream with me

Up a lazy river where the robin's song
Wakes a brand new mornin' as we roll along
There are blue skies up above, and as long as we're in love,
Up a lazy river, how happy we could be,
If you go up a lazy river with me.
I said with me now,
Goin' up that lazy river with me. ❖

WILLIE GILLIS

Norman Rockwell

Back to School

Chapter Three

For millions of service men and women, the return from the war meant not only getting back to work, but also going back to school.

On June 22, 1944, President Franklin D. Roosevelt signed into law the Servicemen's Readjustment Act of 1944, popularly known as the GI Bill of Rights. The GI Bill not only helped veterans with hospitalization costs and the purchase of homes and businesses, it also helped with the cost of higher education.

The federal government subsidized tuition, fees, books and educational materials for veterans and contributed to living expenses incurred while attending college or other approved institutions. The result? In the next seven years, about nine million veterans received educational benefits. By 1951, the GI Bill had cost taxpayers a total of approximately $14 billion.

But what a return on the investment! Higher educational institutions saw a boom of unparalleled proportions. Classrooms and dormitories were bulging with veterans, many of whom could not have dreamed of attending college without the aid of the GI Bill. The new technological economy in the boom years of the 1950s had the GI Bill to thank for training its engineers and technicians. Those boom years were fueled by the brightest minds and strongest backs of "The Greatest Generation."

Veteran students meant an older student body than the characteristic 18- to 23-year-olds. More mature students meant, perhaps, a more serious, studious student body. Colleges and universities also had to expand married student housing as many of the veterans had exchanged vows before shipping out or immediately after returning from European and South Pacific theatres. Veteran villages went up all over America and the complexion of college towns was dramatically changed.

For many, the GI Bill was only part of the back to school picture. They also worked where and when they could to help pay their own way.

I worked three years as a night watchman at a factory in my college town, attending classes through the day, studying when I could and sleeping sporadically. There wasn't much time for a social life, but a special redhead named Janice was waiting for me. I guess I didn't need much socializing.

I think the GI Bill provided an even greater benefit to American society. It allowed us collectively to take a good, deep breath as we adjusted from wartime to peacetime. Education was a constructive way to ease the physical and emotional trauma of war. In its own way the GI Bill allowed us to shake off the tensions of the war years by helping us to get back to school.

—*Ken Tate*

College and the Assembly Line

By Robert J. Miller

The Armed Forces must have been desperate for new recruits in early 1945. That's when my draft board revoked my deferment and ordered me to leave my job as a production expediter in the Philadelphia radar assembly plant of the Philco Corporation. I reported for duty and served in the Army's medical corps until January 1947.

When I sought re-employment at Philco, I was pleasantly surprised when the personnel manager welcomed me back with an apology. He said he was sorry that he couldn't offer me more than $36 a week. While he seemed to be chagrined, I was ecstatic; at the time I was drafted, my salary had been only $23 a week!

The next day I reported for work. I was fortunate to be assigned to the same department I'd left, and was glad that my old supervisor was still in charge. My duties, however, were somewhat different. Instead of building military radar and radio sets, the department was now producing record changers and small table radios.

The challenge was daunting. Earning a college degree at night called for many hours of intensive effort because the program required attendance at class three or four evenings a week.

The postwar era was a time of rapid growth in the electronics industry. Old products were greatly improved and new ones were introduced. Consumers were eager to buy the gadgets they'd been denied during the years of wartime shortages.

Philco's record player department experienced many changes in the race to keep up in the marketplace. Development by Columbia Records of the long-playing disc and by RCA Victor of the 45-rpm record forced the company's engineers to design a series of multiple-speed machines that found favor among consumers. Overtime was plentiful as we worked to meet the demand.

It was while working there that I met two people who greatly influenced me and changed the direction of my life's endeavors. The first person was a young man about my age, who was assigned to a work station next to mine. His name was Clifford.

I found Clifford to be a fascinating character. He was passionate about opera and classical music, and admitted that he had had some training as a musician. During breaks, he and I enjoyed many conversations about various subjects. He acted as a teacher, explaining plots of operas and the nuances of works by the classical composers.

During our discussions, he often told me that he thought I was too smart to waste my life in a factory. He insisted that I should seek to better myself by going into another line of work. Almost every day, Clifford chided me for being content to remain a factory hand. In response, I began to revise my thinking.

One day, Clifford showed me a newspaper ad. It stated that a local college was instituting a degree program for working people by offering night classes. He urged me to consider enrolling.

After much thought, I sent for an application form. When I showed it to Clifford, he assured me that I could meet the admissions criteria and that I could handle the workload. He was right! I took the entrance exams and was accepted as a freshman for the coming fall term. Clifford had made his point, and my life was altered from then on!

Of course, the challenge was daunting. Earning a college degree at night called for many hours of intensive effort because the program required attendance at class three or four evenings a week, with untold hours of study at home and in the library. Somehow, though, with Clifford's encouragement ringing in my ears, I persevered. I was deeply disappointed that he never saw me graduate, however; during the second year, he left Philco to join his father in a refrigeration business. We never saw each other again.

Philco's advertising slogan proclaimed that the company was "Famous for Quality the World Over." But the company's facilities were also famous for the "Philco Romance." Since the workforce was composed mainly of women, most of whom had been hired during the war years, there was plenty of opportunity for romance to develop among the workers. After all, women outnumbered the men by almost two to one.

One day shortly after Clifford's departure, the second Philco-ite who was to alter my life entered the scene. Management decided to centralize production by moving a subassembly department from an outlying plant to the one in which I was working. Among the transferees was a pretty young woman whose work station was close to mine. A few days after her arrival, we were introduced to each other by a fellow employee.

It didn't take long to develop a friendship. As had happened with Clifford, I found myself

I'm the one standing between two barracks mates at Fort Meade, Md., in April 1946.

talking to her almost every day. Eventually I got up the courage to ask her for a date, and much to my surprise, she said, "Yes."

That first date led to another and still more until the lucky day when she responded favorably to a proposal of marriage. And we lived happily thereafter.

What happy events were set in motion by that draft call in 1945! The years that followed were some of the most pleasurable of my life. ❖

This ladies' bowling team won the Philco league championship in 1950. The young lady in the right foreground also won my heart a few years later.

From Tuskegee To Educator

By Robert W. Johnson, as told to Tina M. Hultslander

The Tuskegee experience changed my life. For African-Americans during the 1940s, a good education was hard to achieve. The Tuskegee Institute opened my eyes to the importance of education, and the GI Bill made that possible.

I never saw action in World War II. I was in advanced training at the Division of Aeronautics of Tuskegee Institute when the war ended. I had two choices. I could get my civilian's pilot license from Myerstown, Pa., or I could go to school.

Blacks weren't readily accepted as civilian pilots then, so I knew that if I was ever going to make a difference in the world, or this life, I had to go down the path toward education. During midterm in February 1946, I became a student at Morgan State University in Baltimore, Md.

I liked sports as well as the sciences, so I combined all of my interests into one degree. I graduated in 1950 with a Bachelor of Science in Health, Physical Education and Science.

Robert W. Johnson, 1944

Thanks to the GI Bill, I got my degree, and now I was going to get a job.

I headed for Hagerstown, Md., to become one of the instructors at an all-black school on North Street. I never had heard of Hagerstown before, but I packed my bags and took the bus. When I got there, I approached the only other African-American in the bus terminal. When I asked if he knew where I could stay, he suggested Harmon's Hotel on Jonathan Street, where some of the other teachers from the school were staying.

The school kept me busy. I taught science to the ninth-grade students, biology to the 10th grade and physics and chemistry to the 11th and 12th grades. I was also the physical education instructor for all of them. I saw hope in my new job and looked toward a bright future.

In 1956, when the Washington County school system in Hagerstown, Md., became integrated, I became the first black coach at North Hagerstown High School. Within a few years, I was head of the physical education department. I wanted people to

Robert Johnson, far left, at Morgan State University

know that it wasn't how I looked that should matter, but rather what I knew and what I could share.

I continued to work my way up the education ladder. In 1974, I became the first black administrator in an integrated school system when I accepted the job as vice principal at E. Russell Hicks Middle School.

Because of my education, I was able to work with underprivileged youth in the schools to reassure them that nothing was impossible. If I could achieve my dreams, then so could they. I tried to make an impact on as many children as I could until I retired in 1983.

My life has been good, and the goodness was made possible through the higher education I received from the GI Bill. Without it, I might never have become a respected member of my community, nor would I have been able to positively touch as many young lives as I hope I have. An education gives one the chance to make the world a better place for all, and I have tried to do just that! ❖

Robert Johnson as instructor at North Street School, 1956.

My Cloud's Silver Lining

By Marianna K. Tull

When I graduated from high school in 1939, the serious problems in Europe were not on my list of worries. I was 18 and excited about starting my freshman year of college in the Midwest. Both my parents had migrated to Pennsylvania from the Midwest before I was born, but they wanted me to become acquainted with life in the area they loved. So my freshman and sophomore years were spent at a small junior college in Illinois.

Things were going from bad to worse in Europe, but my main concern was choosing another Midwestern college from which I hoped to get my degree. I spent my last two years at a wonderful college in southern Ohio where the Ohio and Muskingum Rivers meet. As I avidly watched our football games in the fall of 1941, I had not the slightest clue that the six-foot, 200-pound tackle on our team would someday be the father of my two sons.

He was a young man from Baltimore who had chosen this college because several of his close friends were students there.

Midway into my senior year, that 200-pound tackle asked me to be his wife. I had no problem saying "Yes," even though we both knew his college days were numbered. He had enlisted in the Army.

It was a heart-wrenching farewell for both of us when he had to leave. He wound up in a camp down South, but as far as I was concerned, it might as well have been the end of the world. Little did I know!

As I avidly watched our football games in the fall of 1941, I had not the slightest clue that the six-foot, 200-pound tackle on our team would someday be the father of my two sons.

Several months later, he was chosen to go to Officer Candidate School. We were both ecstatic, but things were not going well across the ocean. Young soldiers were being sent overseas fast and furious. I was haunted by the fact that I might never again see this man I loved so much. He was granted a short leave, and thanks to my family, we had a memorable wedding ceremony in my parents' home.

We crammed a lot into that short leave. After two days and nights in one of Philadelphia's finest hotels, it was back on the train to Baltimore to spend the remaining days with his family. His hopes of OCS were shattered when he returned to camp and learned that his unit was to be shipped out in just a few months. We had married in November and he was ordered to go overseas in early August. I was devastated because he was leaving, but ecstatic because I was pregnant.

Somehow he managed to get two hours leave in Philadelphia before leaving New York on the *Queen Mary* for not-so-jolly old England. When my husband saw me, I was *so* pregnant that he said I looked like I was pushing a load of laundry. Better to laugh than cry.

Two weeks later, our son was born. A friend whose husband was a captain in the Merchant Marine was anxious to let my husband know the good news. Our friend was in Scotland and called my husband in England to give him the important news that he had a son.

After dodging bombs in England, my husband was off to the beach in Normandy. His company crossed France to the land of Hitler. My husband distinguished himself on the battlefield, and was proud to have Gen. Patton pin the Bronze Star on his uniform.

When the war finally ended, my husband was sent to Czechoslovakia for a short time. Then the day *finally* came—he was coming home! The trip back on the Liberty ship was not a great one, but you can take almost anything if you are coming home.

Our son knew "Dadee" only by his photograph, but "Dadee" was thrilled when his son accepted him immediately.

Now the GI Bill was to play an important part in our lives, as my husband made plans to go back to college and get his degree in education. He wanted to teach school. My dad gave us a car, and we loaded it with our worldly goods and headed for the Ohio college where we had met.

My husband had made a trip to Ohio a few weeks earlier and had rented a barn of an apartment in town, on the third floor. A furniture store occupied the first floor and the second floor was vacant. We rented the whole third floor for $47 a month. We had three huge rooms, plus a kitchen, bath and huge hallway.

The kitchen contained an ancient gas stove. This was new to me; my mother cooked with electricity. I was terrified of the stove at first, but

we soon became friends, though not easily. There was a large hole in the bottom of the oven. If your cake was too close to the hole, it burned. If it was too far way, part of it was soggy.

The refrigerator looked forward to the iceman every week. A pan under the refrigerator caught the water from the melting ice. The only reminder to empty the pan was a stream of water running across the kitchen floor.

A big potato was a must in our bathroom. Every time the toilet was flushed, a stream of water gushed out of a pipe and the floor became a lake. But my husband soon devised a plan to solve the problem; thereafter, a huge potato was stuck on the end of the pipe to correct the waterfall.

Many of my husband's friends had returned from military service to continue their education, also thanks to the GI Bill. Our apartment soon became the gathering place for this elite group. Our son loved every minute of it, and he became the center of attention. They brought him jigsaw puzzles, books and many other things of interest to a two-year-old.

My husband's boyhood friend from Baltimore had returned to college after serving as a lieutenant in the paratroopers. When he needed a place to stay while he completed his senior year, we offered him part of our large living room. Now we had a new dinner companion, and I think he enjoyed the meals I concocted on that old gas stove. He once told me that I made French fries better than the French!

The GI Bill made these wonderful things possible. Our friendships with these young men lasted a lifetime. They shared an experience not common to all young men. The appreciation and love they felt for this country lasted throughout their lives. The GI Bill enabled my husband to get the degree in education that he wanted so much, and it made it possible for him to enjoy almost 40 years of doing what he loved best: teaching young people.

Yes, I was one of Frankie's swooning fans, and our two sons were captivated by Howdy Doody as well as Kukla, Fran and Ollie. But the best part of those years after the war was knowing that my cloud had a silver lining! ❖

Back to Peace

By Margaret Gunn

It's a pleasure to recall the "coming home" of the guy I loved and was married to for 54 years. However, there were three years in there, after he returned home and before our courtship and marriage.

Bill Gunn delayed his homecoming from France to attend Biarritz American University in Biarritz, France, for a summer. He had accumulated enough points for his discharge, but he felt that the chance to get college credit in that beautiful place before he headed back to the States was a wonderful opportunity. His mother was not happy about this decision; naturally, she wanted her boy safely home. However, she understood that the experience was important to Bill.

Imagine our joy when he and I revisited that lovely place for our 50th wedding anniversary. I was so excited about the visit that I wrote about it for our local paper. The day after the article appeared, we received two urgent phone calls from men eager to talk with Bill. They, too, had been in Biarritz, so the fellows got together and shared memories.

But I'm getting ahead of myself. When Bill returned safely to our hometown of Galena, Ill., I was delighted. We'd been good friends in high school, and I liked Bill a lot. We later realized it was more than "like," but at the time, we were both busy with our lives.

I worked in the local bank. Before embarking on his academic pursuits, Bill had worked at an ordnance station in a neighboring town. He had done this before the war, during high-school summers, and he often said he had gotten the equipment out before the war and helped put it away when peace came.

Then it was off to college for Bill—Michigan State University. He had had a year of college at a school in southern Illinois before going to Europe to serve, and also had credits from the Biarritz experience. For the next two years at MSU, he lived in a "hut" on campus with fellow veterans who remained our friends for many years.

During his time on campus, he worked part time. He was busy, of course, but he got to Galena from time to time. And that's when our romance blossomed. As a good high-school friend, I had sent him cookies while he was in the Army. Later he told me it was those cookies that did it!

On one of his trips from campus, Bill had a little box, and inside it was a diamond ring. He wondered if I would wear it. Would I?! I'm *still* wearing that diamond!

Then it was wedding time for us. Bill graduated from the university one week and got married the next. He said he got his bachelor's one week and lost his bachelor status the next. He planned to pursue a graduate degree at MSU, so after a week in Chicago and a few weeks back in Galena, we were off for the campus that had been part of his life for the years after the war. We lived in a trailer in college housing, and our neighbors were like us—the fellows were veterans. We often said we were all in the same boat—"sometimes a leaky one."

Babies flourished in that place, and we joined the crowd on that, too, having our first baby while Bill was still a student. But we, like our friends, survived! Two other babies followed our firstborn, and one of our sons is named Ron. Bill had seen his good Army buddy Ron crash in a flaming plane in France. He resolved that if he had a son, he would name him after his friend.

I read of World War II veterans dying daily; Bill became a part of that group at age 80. Here again, the Army looms: His burial place is in Fort Custer National Cemetery. It's a beautiful spot, and many of our friends are there. It's inspiring to visit that place. The flags fly—the flags for this great, great country, for which so many fought bravely. ❖

Things Aren't Always As They Seem

By Eleanor Donica

I went to a cousin's funeral the other day, and Jessie was there. We hugged and shared another laugh about the worry I caused her long ago.

I graduated from Monett (Mo.) High School in May 1943 and went right into nurse's training. Since I was a Baptist and the Southern Baptist Hospital accepted me as a student, I went to New Orleans for my training. So when I went away from home for the first time, I went a long way away.

My daddy worked for the Frisco Railroad, and each year he was given a number of "foreign passes" to use on another rail service. I used one of those passes to take the Kansas City Southern's *Southern Belle Special* from Neosho, Mo., to New Orleans.

I remember waving to Daddy as I boarded the Frisco. He was switching in the yards that day. I am sure his heart must have been breaking to see me go alone to my destiny. No one took me on the 30-mile journey to Neosho to catch the *Southern Belle*. I left Monett on my own.

We were poor (and didn't know it), but my education was very inexpensive. The tuition was $25 plus a $10 breakage deposit. We worked for our room, board, uniforms and teaching. The hospital didn't have nurses' aides—just students with registered nurses acting as the floor supervisors.

I suppose I must have gotten homesick during my training. There were no phone calls; there wasn't enough money for that. Only in cases of emergency did you make or receive a phone call. Stamps were three cents then, but I doubt that Mom or I had much time to write letters.

One day I was downtown on Canal Street with one of my classmates. I was in the Woolworth store—on the right side of the street, going from the Mississippi River. (I never knew directions when I lived in New Orleans; I just followed the street signs.)

We were probably enjoying some free fun riding the escalator. I had never had that chance before and I always rode it a few extra times when I could.

I looked over the crowd, and there stood a sailor! I always loved sailor suits more than the other uniforms. There he stood, tall, handsome—my very own cousin, Leon. I must have really loved him up! But there stood Jessie, his wife, looking at me! Leon introduced me as his cousin, which was the truth, but I guess it was a bad situation.

"A likely story," she accused him. "A girl in every port!" Poor man. He had to write home and have his mother write and tell Jessie that he really did have a cousin in New Orleans.

Years later, long after the war was over, I found out that they had been shopping for a clock so she could get him to the ship on time. When I met up with them, she thought she had discovered that he'd been cheating on her.

Leon still has pretty blue eyes. He is skinny now, and stooped, but Jessie still loves him. We have a good laugh every time we see one another. So you see, things aren't always as they seem. ❖

College Wife

By Mary McClintock

I came to the United States as a GI bride in May 1946, having been married in London in 1944. My husband was working on his master's degree at the University of Illinois in Urbana, and I started work in the recorder's office and as a secretary to the Committee on Student Discipline.

How different office work was then! For one thing, the boss was never called by his first name. I banged away on a manual typewriter with no handy helpers like correction fluid or film to erase mistakes. Errors had to be painfully removed with a type eraser, first inserting scraps of paper in the appropriate placed on all the carbon copies; the carbons had to be erased individually.

If a typist made a really big mistake, like omitting a paragraph, the whole thing had to be redone. This always seemed to happen with particularly long letters. The process of just making room for the missing paragraph and inserting it would not have been believed by secretaries in those computerless days.

I took verbatim shorthand minutes of the committee's meetings, and woe betide me if there was something I could not read back, because no one else in the office used Pitman shorthand, and there were no tape recorders.

The committee was very interesting to work for; but if such a body exists these days, it must have some heinous crimes to deal with. The things for which students were called on the carpet back then are just a part of everyday college life now. The concepts of coed dorms and the freedom to come and go at all hours would have amazed students in 1946.

Since this was very soon after World War II, many of the students were older than usual, married, and existing on money provided under the GI Bill. This was the case for us, too. It wasn't easy, even with one spouse working.

At the end of the month, my husband and I would celebrate by going out for coffee together. Occasionally we shared a milkshake—one drink, two straws—at a shop run by a local dairy. They were the best milkshakes I have ever had, made with whole milk and the dairy's creamiest ice cream. It was a blue-ribbon event for us, which started with a stroll of several blocks on a warm summer evening, with fireflies darting and katydids singing. We never thought of being mugged.

During the first part of our time at the university, we lived in two small rooms at the top of a house and shared a bathroom. We had an icebox, which was new to me. I forgot to empty the pan on several occasions, and the water ended up in the apartment below.

Life directly under the roof in an Illinois summer is sweltering, so we installed a big exhaust fan in the kitchen window. We had to batten down the hatches before turning it on, though, as this monster seemed capable of sucking the tablecloth and its contents right off the table!

Our small gas-cooker oven had no thermostat, so we bought one and stood it on the rack. We also bought an old treadle sewing machine. I had never sewn before except for embroidery, but that ancient machine turned out a lot of sun suits, small shorts and window curtains, once we came to understand each other. At first I had trouble coordinating the action of my foot

Usually the husbands were studying when they were not in class, and in the evenings, the wives practiced being very quiet and keeping the baby, if there was one, quiet too.

with the rhythm of the treadle; I thought I never would learn.

All our friends were married couples, but we seldom got together except for an occasional picnic, which was the least expensive form of entertainment. Usually the husbands were studying when they were not in class, and in the evenings, the wives practiced being very quiet and keeping the baby, if there was one, quiet too.

We had a baby daughter in 1947, and eventually got a tiny house in Illini Village, the university's housing project for married students. This was a great relief after our stint in the attic.

Life with a baby was very different back then. Now there are disposable diapers and feeding bottles, and many things to make life easier, including modern washers and dryers and permanent-press clothes.

I washed mostly in our single sink, although at one time we did have a very small and inadequate tabletop washer. My first real washing machine, after we left the university, was an Easy, with three large, metal, suction cups that pounded up and down on the clothes. It did a very good job.

As for ironing, 14 or 15 little dresses, all with puffed sleeves and ribbons and frills, were on the ironing board every week, along with small jackets, nightwear, shawls and sheets, plus my husband's and my clothes.

We lived in fear of polio outbreaks every summer. Today's mothers have much to thank Dr. Salk for. Our "bible" was Dr. Spock's book, *Baby and Child Care*. Every young mother had one. I wore one out completely, and still have the second one, minus its cover and with many loose pages held together by a rubber band.

Well, we were young, and it was all rather an adventure. Now we can be comfortably nostalgic about it. Those were the Good Old Days, perhaps seen through a slightly rose-colored haze. ❖

College Girl of the 1940s

By Janis Fedor

The year was 1949. I was the first female in my family to attend college. Upon entering the all-girl dormitory, my new roommate and I were handed a list of "thou-shalt-nots," which were to serve as written parents "in absentia."

We were not to smoke in our room; a smoking room was provided in the basement for those in need. As I was a nonsmoker, this presented no problem for me. We were permitted no electrical appliances. (How would present-day college girls cope without computer, hair dryer, curling iron, radio, CD player and TV?)

Before we could even leave the building, we had to register in a sign-out book kept in the housemother's room. We had to be in our rooms during the week at 9 p.m. sharp, 10 p.m. on weekends. Upperclasswomen were permitted to stay out until 11 p.m. Lights in our room had to be out by 10 p.m., and cheating with flashlights in closets was strictly prohibited, regardless of how far behind one was in her studies.

Under no circumstances was a female college student permitted to ride in a car. Nor could she drive a car, even if she owned it. She could not "hitch rides" with any male college students (who *were* permitted to own and drive vehicles), or—especially—with the town boys.

Saturday afternoon teas took place in each dormitory's lounge lobby. Young ladies were expected to wear modest, black-veiled hats, white gloves and their best dresses.

Sundays, we were expected to be present at a church of our choice off campus. If we did not attend, the housemother would note that we had not signed out for church. Then as soon as she could, she would bestow upon us her best scowl.

This was a teacher's college run by the state. As a rule, up until World War II, teacher's colleges had been attended mostly by females. Now, with World War II over, many veterans were attending institutions of higher learning because the government was paying for their tuition. But even with so many GIs attending our college, there was still a substantial shortage of male companionship. Our Saturday-night dances took place from 6–8 p.m. in the dormitory ballroom where, for the most part, girls danced with girls.

This was, however, where I met the man I would marry—an ex-Navy man.

Despite the rigid rules, we girls had a way around it all. Many nights we lived on the cutting edge of danger by staying out beyond curfew. We got to know the schedules of the hired watchmen and then sneaked back into the dorm at a later hour. We even dared to hike outside the city limits, where we were forbidden to go, and we went roller-skating at the skating rink.

As dormitory students, we were expected to eat in the communal dining hall, but I rarely ate there. Mom's good cooking had spoiled me. I got a part-time job earning 35 cents an hour stapling together a weekly advertising pamphlet. My future husband and I and about eight others sat around a rotating wheel on which the pages were laid out. We got hysterical after a while, trying to keep from missing a page if the wheel turned too fast. But I was able to eat out a lot, thanks to that job.

I made a little extra money, too, by helping some of the GIs write term papers. Had it not been for their war benefits, many might never have considered attending college. Some of them could scarcely read, let alone write.

Now, I wonder: Would modern college students consider going back in time and attending the college of my day? Males, don't reply; you've *always* been liberated! ❖

Crime Wave in Veterans' Village

By Ann T. Cook

N o guns," my husband said, tapping the table for emphasis. "We won't need guns."

A hulking veteran in dungarees beside him nodded. "We've got enough men. We'll nail him with our bare fists."

The tiny living and dining area of our trailer swarmed that November night with angry men, vowing to rid the community of a common menace. The year was 1948, and the place was Trailerville, Eastern Illinois State College in Charleston, Ill.—one of hundreds of veterans' villages that had sprung up on college campuses after World War II.

In one of the best investments the government ever made, it paid its veterans to earn an education. Almost $100 per month went to married men. When hoards of eager enrollees stormed the campuses and overwhelmed housing facilities, trailers, metal huts and converted barracks blossomed within college communities in every state.

My husband, recently discharged from the Navy, had been elated to find a college that would register yet another ex-serviceman, and doubly pleased that we could move with our infant daughter into an expandable trailer in its veterans' village. But several months later, a crisis had brought a posse to our home.

For the past three weeks, a peeping tom had been tormenting Trailerville. Several wives worked a night shift at a local factory. When they returned in the early morning hours to undress for bed, they had become unwitting lures.

Trailerville husbands and wives found evidence of the peeper—footprints and the barrel he stood on at the windows. Although the police were notified, each time a patrol car roared up with siren blasting, the intruder failed to appear.

The outraged husbands determined to take charge. That night, 10 men had been trusted with the suspect's capture; William Garner, the mayor; my husband, Jim; the fire chief, Charles Compton; James Jones; James Moritz, crewcut Elmo Hildebrand; burly Gunboat LaRose; and three others, all eager to lay their hands on the man they saw as a sex fiend.

A trap was set. The steel barrel near the trailers' high windows would

A shout rang out. Up popped the garbage can lid, and out popped the barrel of a gun. A weapon bristled from behind every bush and around every corner.

be set aside. One of the smaller men would conceal himself in a garbage can. Others would hide behind shrubs, around trailer corners and under garbage racks. When the culprit appeared, they would spring the trap.

Rumors had circulated that he was a big man. Although no one knew if he carried a gun, they all agreed to remain unarmed. They would pound him into submission. Each hungered for the first punch, and none doubted that an epic battle lay ahead.

Before midnight, they took their places. The night-shift wives were to act as bait. Time dragged. Finally, at 1:30 a.m., a man in a dark suit and broad-brimmed hat slipped out of the shadows. Seeing his customary footrest removed, he seized a lawn chair, planted it under a window and climbed into position.

A shout rang out. Up popped the garbage can lid, and out popped the barrel of a gun. A weapon bristled from behind every bush and around every corner. As it turned out, each man in the posse was packing his war souvenir .38 or .45, just in case.

But the artillery was not needed. The sagging captive collapsed. He was a slight, pathetic figure, a clerk in a downtown men's store. He told a sad tale: He had a large, domineering wife; he would never hurt anybody;

he had a psychological problem; he needed help.

In that kinder, gentler year, the group's rage subsided. Four of them took the offender off to a city jail, where he was held for a time, then freed on bond. We agreed not to press for a heavy penalty if he agreed to accept counseling. Several stories of the veterans' exploit appeared in the local newspaper, and then we settled back into our trusting way of life.

It was an era when colleges enrolled veterans, trusting them to pay when their GI checks arrived, when doctors delivered babies on the cuff and hospitals let couples take care of bills in installments.

Even the local bank opened an account for my husband and placed funds in it, taking his word that he would repay the loan. He did. The veterans achieved a record of honesty that matched the town's spirit of compassion.

Perhaps that spirit affected 10 vengeful veterans on that November night. At least the experience foreshadowed my husband's future. After a peeping tom turned Jim's righteous anger into pity, he launched a 40-year career in delinquency prevention and jail management— a career in which rehabilitation was always more important than retribution. ❖

My Wartime Vow

By Charley Sampsell

As I sat alone in the operations office of the 409th Base Group at the Clovis, N.M., Army Air Field on a starry, moonlit, early spring night in 1944, I thought about my situation and about my future. My first year in the Air Force had moved me from one organization and air base to another too frequently for me to detect any hint of a purpose or plan. I was 19 years old, without a friend, and farther from my home in southwest Michigan than I had ever been before.

My loneliness, homesickness and a sense of foreboding were overwhelming. Shortly before our planes returned in the early morning, I turned my tired eyes upward and took a solemn oath. "Dear God," I vowed, "if you could please get me back home to Michigan, I will never leave again."

I felt a lot better immediately. I had done about all I could to straighten things out. Two years later, God kept his part of the bargain as I departed the separation center at Fort Sheridan, Ill., and caught the Twilight Limited train from Chicago for my ride home to Kalamazoo, Mich. The scenery became more familiar with every mile. I had every intention of keeping my oath never to leave home.

I returned to live with my semiretired parents on their 80-acre farm near Kalamazoo. For the next two years, life, liberty and the pursuit of happiness were wonderful. There was very little lacking in my life during those years. Eventually, like most returning veterans, I began to look for a promising job, a new car and someone with whom I could share the rest of my life. I found the car first, then a job in a factory only five miles from my parents' farm. At work, I soon met a wonderful young lady named Delores. Within months we married and began looking for a home to buy in town.

Fate then dealt us a complete change of plans by closing the factory in which we were both employed. Before our unemployment benefits had expired, we decided I should use the GI Bill to go to college and become an accountant. We chose Michigan State University at East Lansing, about 75 miles away. My oath to never leave home was seriously threatened for the first time. We sidestepped the issue by living in a trailer at college and commuting to my parents' farm every Friday night. We spent our Sundays with my wife's large family nearby. We still felt like we had not left home, but were only "boarding out" during the work week.

Four years later, I had earned a Master of Arts degree in accounting and we had gained a two-year-old son named Phil and a new car. We were ready to go home to stay. But there was still one small problem. Employment opportunities for newly formed accountants were in short supply in Kalamazoo. My best prospect was a job as a state tax collector in Grand Rapids, Mich., about 50 miles away.

When necessity forced us to the point of accepting that offer, a kindly professor at MSU heard of the situation and interceded on my behalf with the certified public accounting firm of Ernst & Ernst. His efforts gained me an interview and a job offer from the company's Kalamazoo office. We were ecstatic and accepted the offer immediately.

Just after Christmas in 1953, we drove to Kalamazoo, found a $75-per-month apartment, and rented a truck to return to East Lansing and load up our meager possessions—a sofa and chair, a bed, a kitchen table and chairs, a child's crib and a couple of dressers, in the van.

Soon we were rolling south on M-78, heading home to Kalamazoo. As we neared the end of our journey, I looked into the beautiful southwest Michigan sunset and said, "Thank you, God, for bringing us back to our home again. We will never leave it."

Fifty years later, we have not. ❖

College Years

By M.E. Smith

Sunday, Sept. 16, 1945
Goodbyes had been said, and Mother and Dad had driven away. I knew they would talk about me as they drove home. They would reassure each other that they had every right to have faith in me and hope for my future. This was what they had worked for, and now, amid the joy of doing it, there was sadness in the loss of my presence.

Always they had known that this was the way of life. Children grow and children leave home. Mother, the baby in her family, had seen her brothers leave one by one as she grew up. Dad had taught other boys who worked for him in the market and had seen them go on to other things.

Mom and Dad were concerned but not fearful. They loved and trusted me, but I was their only treasure. Most of their married life had revolved lovingly around me, and now they were driving away and leaving their only child. Mother had raised a little boy and Dad had pointed him to become a man, but I wasn't there yet, and they knew it. Now, in faith, they had left me alone in a world that was strange to me and to them. This was a bigger town, and I was about to embark on college life.

So very often I had heard Mother say, "Melvin, if there is a way, you are going to college." The time had arrived for which she had worked and dreamed, teaching me my ABCs, helping me night after night to learn my spelling, and holding one end of a string while I swung the lines of latitude to draw a map of the United States on the dining-room table. Now she would not be there to hold the string.

The next morning, I made my bed, dressed and went in search of breakfast. The Jayhawk across the street was closed, not yet open for the fall semester. I went up on "The Hill" to the Cottage Café. It was nice to look out across the valleys of the Wakarusa and the Kaw. This campus sure was different from the flatlands around my hometown of Moran, Kan.

I was almost alone. I had arrived early because Dad could leave the City Meat Market only on Sunday afternoons. At the Cottage, music was playing. It was *Mockingbird Hill* by Les Paul and Mary

> **There were about three girls for every boy that first semester. Most fraternities were closed for lack of boys, or were being used as girls' dormitories.**

Ford. I remember it well, and the waitress, whom I would date six years later.

There were about three girls for every boy that first semester. Most fraternities were closed for lack of boys, or were being used as girls' dormitories. Most of the girls looked like they had just got out of bed and thrown on any old thing before they trudged to class.

The second semester was different. Now the GIs were back, and suddenly there were four or five boys for every girl. That sure made a difference in the way the girls dressed and dolled up.

And now my classes were crowded with returning servicemen. At first they were rusty and slow—almost bewildered. But after a few weeks, they were engaged in serious competition for the top grades. I was impressed. I had thought I was there on business, but these guys showed me what it really meant to be there for a purpose.

Housing became a problem. For the married GIs, converted Army barracks blossomed on flat land south of the campus. We called it "Pregnant Prairie."

My first year cost Dad $800, almost to the penny. Having worked for him, I knew that a year's income above our living was about $1,000, and now Dad had to hire someone to replace me. I knew how hard Dad worked for his money, that there was no pension for him, and he needed more savings than he had. I enlisted in the Army for two years so I could finish my college on the GI Bill, with no further expense to Dad.

In the fall of 1948, I was back. Many students in my classes were almost as green as I once had been. Most of the returning GIs now were in the upper classes. I attended class dressed in surplus Army gear. I was no longer a timid, small-town kid who had been growing up slowly. I did not think of myself as a man yet—one must be earning his own living for that—but having been a sergeant in charge of the editing section of a photomapping company in Tokyo, my former bashfulness had been replaced by confidence.

My knowledge of the meat business, learned back home under Dad's tutelage, and the confidence and maturity I had gained in the Army benefited me in college, especially in speech class. As a junior, I found myself in an elective two-hour-credit speech class with a bunch of freshmen, and a pretty, intelligent, but inexperienced young female teacher. My other 17 credit hours of chemical engineering courses took priority, and I dealt with that speech class with the back of my left hand.

Suddenly, in class one day, I realized that we were to give a brief lesson using the blackboard and a simple freehand drawing. My presentation was impromptu, but the teacher never knew it. I sketched the front quarter of a beef and described the first cuts to "open up" the quarter for further subdivision into steaks and roasts. It was a piece of cake—er, meat.

But that was not the end of my fun with that attractive, newly married teacher. One day she asked each of us to give a sentence illustrating the differences in meaning that could be expressed by accentuating different words, or groups of words, in the sentence. When my turn came, her head was down, as she was writing comments on the last student's performance in her notebook. As straight as I could say it, I asked, "Can I have a date next Saturday?"

Lost somewhere in thought, she seemed to give my question serious consideration as she replied, "Uh, well …." When she suddenly realized where she was, she blushed red while the class roared with laughter.

That sentence *can* be meant different ways.

Just before finals, that sweet young teacher announced that the final test would be over the book. What a low blow! I had been impromptu all semester, and my heavy chemical engineering courses demanded serious study for finals. What to do? Well, the book must at least be scanned—and fast.

The paragraphs were long and dull, but shortly I noted that each started with a well-written opening sentence; if you understood that sentence, the rest of the paragraph was a waste of time. I finished the book in about an hour. In the Army, I had learned to meet deadlines.

I got an "A" in the course—but no date with the teacher. ❖

Marching Back To Class

By Carrol C. Lowe

In November 1945, I bid farewell to the U.S. Navy and mentally prepared myself for the civilian world that awaited my family and me.

During World War II, I had gained combat experience, a lovely wife and a beautiful baby daughter. My temporary homes for the past few years had been aboard the battleship *Texas,* the destroyer *Brownson,* and a sub chaser that I boarded in Panama. While ashore, I had lived in barracks and naval housing in New York; Texas; Norfolk, Va.; San Francisco, Calif.; Miami and Hollywood Beach, Fla., and Cape May, N.J.

Now, in November 1945, my family and I were housed in a small, austere hotel near the Great Lakes Naval Center, Chicago, where I was being processed and released to inactive duty. All our worldly possessions were in a wooden box that had come with us on the train from Norfolk, Va., a few days earlier.

While my friends and I studied and took exams, our families gossiped, played cards, drank coffee and played with the children.

Our hotel had a bathroom down the hall. The whole atmosphere of the place was far from hospitable. My wife and baby spent the long days there while I was being processed, and we were together at night.

After the Navy presented me with a huge $100 gift, we boarded a train for my home in Oblong, Ill. For a time, we lived in southern Illinois, and ultimately I was accepted for school under the GI Bill of Rights by Peabody-Vanderbilt University at Nashville, Tenn.

Officially I pursued courses leading to a master's degree at Peabody, but part of my classes were at Vanderbilt University. (These educational institutions were to merge some time later.) We were promised veterans housing, but it was not yet ready when we arrived, so we secured a room in an old house owned by a retired schoolteacher.

My mother sent canned blackberries, green beans and other staples with us so that we and her only grandchild would not starve. We received a $90 stipend from the government and matched that with an equal amount from our savings, which consisted of savings bonds that we had purchased through withholdings from our salaries.

The old house was dirty and somewhat run-down. Our landlady blamed it all on the fact that the servants had left to secure higher-paying jobs in the defense industry. She had never done menial work and did not intend to start now.

While I attended classes about 12 blocks away, my wife scrubbed down the room where we lived, as well as the hall and steps leading to the front door. She purchased cheap, colorful material for curtains and red linoleum for the floor. Our "oasis in the desert" was so inviting that the landlady and her sister visited often and stayed long. Of course, they insisted that they came to see our beautiful baby; however, they complimented my wife on her beautiful room.

After four or five months, we were able to move into the veterans housing complex. By now I was well on my way toward earning my master's degree and securing a teacher's certificate. The housing consisted of family units within a barracks-type building. The furniture was not expensive, but it was new, and we were delighted with the arrangement.

Living space was hard to find after the war. Right after we married, we had been forced to live in a remodeled tourist cabin. Before that, a lady had offered to hang a blanket across the middle of a long room in Miami, Fla., so another couple and we could live there with at least a minimum of privacy.

Life in the veterans housing unit was informal and pleasant. While my friends and I studied and took exams, our families gossiped, played cards, drank coffee and played with the children. Now and then we put our leftovers together and had a "housing picnic." None of us had an appreciable amount of money or material possessions, but we had shared a Depression and a war, and we were very glad to be alive. We were young and looked forward to a future that was brighter than the past few years had been.

However, 1946 still found us in humble circumstances. We did not have a car, and neither did our friends. (Cars were not yet available; the manufacturers had been busy producing tanks and armored vehicles.) So even during cold weather, we walked Nashville's streets as soot rained down on us like large, black snowflakes. The soot was a byproduct of the soft coal that was used to heat so many homes in those days.

One evening my wife and I pushed our baby stroller about 10 blocks to a basketball game that I had to attend as part of my physical education course. But since we did not have enough money for the two of us to attend, I stayed to audit the game and my wife pushed our baby back home. (After all, I needed the credit, so we did what we had to do.)

Finally I finished my studies and received my degree and a teacher's certificate. By now our baby was a beautiful little girl. We bid adieu to our many friends in the housing complex and entered civilian life to pursue the American dream that so many of us had risked our lives to defend. By now we had depleted our supply of war savings bonds, which, along with our $90 from the government, had carried us through. And so we embarked on a teaching and coaching career without a car or financial reserves.

But life was good and the future was bright. I was offered a job for $2,100 per year. I would coach basketball, baseball and track while teaching social studies, history and driver's training.

Once again, however, there was no housing available in the small town where I was to teach. Eventually we took up residence on the edge of town with a lady whose husband had died and whose son was in the service. We had a separate bedroom, but otherwise we lived with her and cooked in her kitchen. However, she worshiped our little girl, and that helped make the situation livable.

I walked to school each morning. When I had to coach a basketball game at night, my family and I walked to the gym. Finally, in the middle of the year, we purchased an old, beat-up car. It was all we could afford—and besides, there were very few cars available.

But our purchase turned into a personal humiliation one day while I was teaching classroom driver training. Some of the students in my class looked down from the second-floor windows and excitedly exclaimed, "Coach, your wife has knocked down the stop sign out in front and the car is resting on top of it!" My students never let me forget that!

The GI Bill made my years teaching and coaching possible. Now, nearly 60 years later, I realize that marching back to class after World War II was the genesis of the best years of our lives. ❖

New Directions

By Warren Dowling

Nov. 14, 1945, was a mile marker in my life. After four years I was a civilian again. During my four years in the service, I spent two in the States and two in the South Pacific. During those years, I had gone where I was told to go and followed orders. Now I was again free to make up my own mind as to what was best for me.

While stationed in Los Angeles in 1942, I had married my childhood sweetheart, Veetrice Mote. After my two years in the South Pacific, we were anxious to start our marriage over again. We were both in our early 20s, with a whole life ahead of us.

Both our families had been involved in farming back as far as we had a record. But we immediately ruled out farming. Our folks had made just a bare living; we wanted something better.

We soon learned that through the GI Bill of Rights, many avenues were open to us. In the history of the world, no government has ever opened up more opportunities to returning soldiers. Under the GI Bill of Rights, I could receive two years of on-the-job training to learn a skill, or I could go to college for four years.

Veetrice and I also had something that most returning servicemen did not have. While I was overseas, Veetrice had worked in Portland, Ore., at a defense plant and had saved several thousand dollars that I had sent as an allotment.

We spent my first month back home just getting to know each other again and trying to decide what direction we wanted to take. A for-

The same GI Bill that offered such a fine opportunity to me also enabled millions of returning service personnel to buy homes with guarantees from the government.

mer teacher urged me to go to college; however, my father had always envisioned his children following in his footsteps. (In fact, he thought the proper wedding gift for a young married couple was a pair of mules.) My younger brother Lester and I had finished high school, but none of my other siblings had even finished grammar school. With this background, I felt like I had been near the bottom of the economic and social ladder. I couldn't see myself as a college graduate.

Besides, Veetrice and I felt like we already had postponed normal life for the four years I had been away. Four more years of college was simply more than I wanted to undertake. We finally decided that I would go to work where I had worked before the war, at the Williams Auto Company of Woodward, Okla.

And so, on Jan. 2, 1946, I started back to work at my old job. I was paid in part by the automobile dealer and in part by Uncle Sam. I worked there until I became a journeyman mechanic.

Veetrice and I were reasonably happy with the job. But we knew that much of the country offered better wages and working conditions than we had in Oklahoma. Also, we couldn't forget the dust storms we had experienced there during "the Dirty Thirties."

One day when I came home from work, I said, "Veetrice, let's move to the West Coast."

"When do we go?" she replied. We took off with no clear destination in mind. We were in Arcata, Calif., near the Oregon border, before I applied for a job at Sacchi Chevrolet. When I told the owner about my qualifications, he wanted me to go to work that afternoon.

I rolled my toolbox in at 8 a.m. the next day, and I worked there for 30 years. The place and I were a perfect fit. And while I was there, I completed enough schooling that I could paper my bedroom wall with the certificates. I also earned a plaque that reads, "30 Years Master Mechanic."

I don't know what my life would have been like without my years in the service and the on-the-job training I was awarded through the GI Bill of Rights. I might still be in Oklahoma picking cotton.

The same GI Bill that offered such a fine opportunity to me also enabled millions of returning service personnel to buy homes with guarantees from the government.

As I write about all the benefits I received from the government, I realize that not all servicemen were so lucky. Many men lost their lives; some were permanently injured. War is never a good thing. But I also know that those of us who did return in good shape received help from our country that gave us a good start in life and allowed us to enjoy a higher standard of living than any generation before us.

In Tom Brokaw's book about the war and its aftermath, he calls us *The Greatest Generation.* I don't know about that, but I do know that we had better jobs and living conditions than any generation before, and it is possible that we were better off than any generation will be in the future. ❖

A mechanic's garage as it appeared in 1959. Photo by Carl Iwasaki Time Life Pictures/Getty Images

College Fight Songs

When we went back to school, college life pulled us to the gridiron. Remember the fight songs that roused everyone for the Saturday football games? Here are three examples from Notre Dame, Michigan and Ohio State.

Notre Dame Fight Song

Cheer, cheer for Old Notre Dame
Wake up the echoes cheering her name,
Send the volley cheer on high,
Shake down the thunder from the sky,
What tho the odds be great or small
Old Notre Dame will win over all,
While her loyal sons are marching
Onward to Victory.

The Yellow & the Blue
Michigan Fight Song

Now for a cheer they are here, triumphant!
Here they come with banners flying,
In stalwart step they're nighing,
With shouts of vict'ry crying,
We hurrah, hurrah, we greet you now,
Hail!

Far we their praises sing
For the glory and fame they've bro't us
Loud let the bells them ring
For here they come with banners flying
Far we their praises tell
For the glory and fame they've bro't us
Loud let the bells them ring
For here they come with banners flying
Here they come, Hurrah!

Hail! to the victors valiant
Hail! to the conqu'ring heroes

Hail! Hail! to Michigan
the leaders and best
Hail! to the victors valiant
Hail! to the conqu'ring heroes
Hail! Hail! to Michigan,
the champions of the West!

We cheer them again
We cheer and cheer again
For Michigan, we cheer for Michigan
We cheer with might and main
We cheer, cheer, cheer
With might and main we cheer!

Hail! to the victors valiant
Hail! to the conqu'ring heroes
Hail! Hail! to Michigan,
the champions of the West!

Buckeye Battle Cry
Ohio State Fight Song

In old Ohio there's a team
That's known throughout the land
Eleven warriors brave and bold,
Whose fame will ever stand.
And when the ball goes over,
Our cheers will reach the sky,
Ohio Field will hear again
The Buckeye Battle Cry!

Drive, drive on down the field,
Men of the scarlet and gray;
Don't let them through that line,
We've got to win this game today,
Come on, Ohio!
Smash through to victory,
We cheer you as you go!
Our honor defend we will fight to
the end for Ohio! ❖

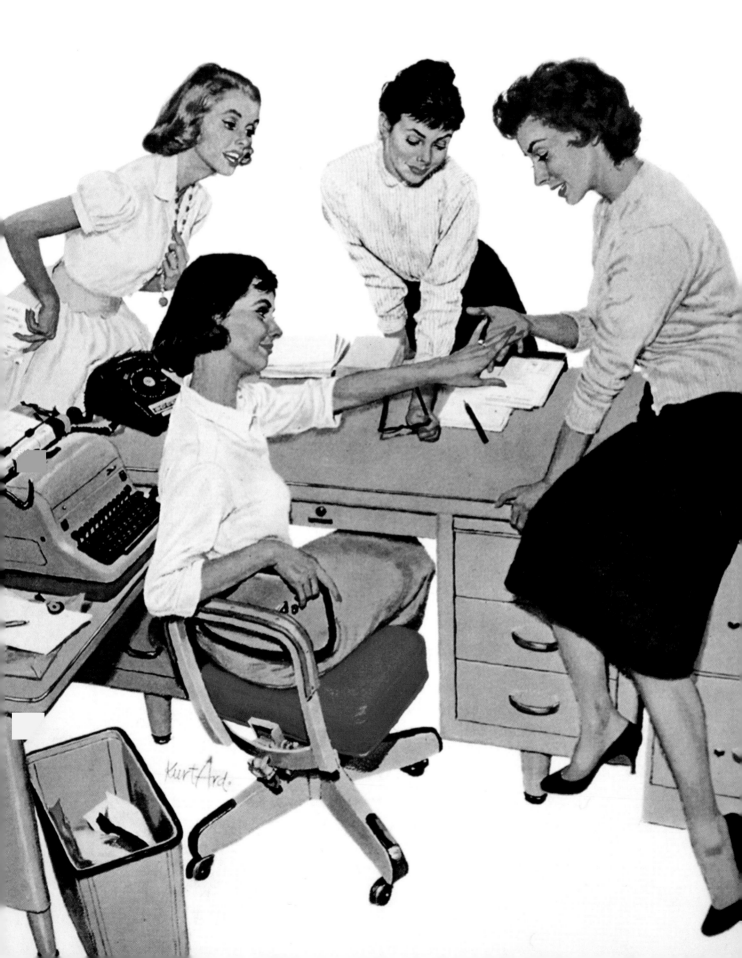

Wedding Bells

Chapter Four

A few years back I read that the record number of golden wedding anniversaries was set in 1996. That didn't surprise me. After all, 50 years before that was the year following the end of World War II. That was the year of wedding bells rang for millions of us. The end of war, a booming economy and now weddings—is it any wonder those were the best years of our lives?

I can't say exactly how wedding bells chimed for anybody else, but the ones that tolled for Janice and me began in front of a small church not far from her home. We had dated a scant five months, but there was no doubt in my mind that this vivacious 18-year-old redhead was my destiny.

I had pulled together every penny I could to afford the engagement ring I gave her that Sunday evening. An engagement ring in itself was a bit of a novelty. Neither of our mothers had had one, but those boom years seemed to beg for things our parents could never afford.

She said she would think about it, but she took the ring with her. I took that as a good sign.

In those days it would have been protocol for me to ask her father for her hand in marriage. I told her I would, if she agreed to be my blushing bride, but I wasn't exactly looking forward to that prospect. To be honest, he scared me to death.

This farmer father of an only child guarded his daughter with a ferocity that would make strong men quake. Janice's male classmates told me unabashedly that they had been afraid to ask her for a date. Attending school a county away, and being three years her senior, made me ignorant of the threat, not necessarily brave enough to face it.

One time in our early dating I brought my redhead home a bit later than I had told her father to expect us. I honestly thought he would shoot me before I left that evening. The transgression never recurred.

Janice took the ring home with her and hid it in a bureau drawer. She only took it out the next couple of weeks to show some of the girls where she worked. She never expected her mother needing something from said drawer and finding the ring. The cat was out of the bag, but I was about to be put in it with a load of rocks and dropped in the nearest creek. Janice didn't even have a phone to give me a warning call to clear out.

The fact that, decades later, I'm still breathing is a testimony that my future father-in-law was more interested in his daughter's happiness than my hide. He still carried a gruff demeanor until well after the wedding, but later became like a second father to me.

Through the boom years that followed, Janice and I gave her father and mother their only three grandchildren. He was the greatest grandfather I could have ever wanted for our children—especially for our two daughters. Those wedding bells that chimed for Janice and me back in the Good Old Days rang in the best years of our lives.

—Ken Tate

MARRIAGE LICENSES

11

norman rockwell

It Must Be Love

By Francis G. Morrison

The greatest day of my life in the greatest year of my life was Nov. 12, 1945. That was the day Millie and I were married.

It was in New York. My ship, a Navy troop transport, was in port for a week, preparing for a trip to Calcutta and back that would take about two months.

I had written to my girl, who was also in the Navy and stationed in Florida. I asked her to try and get leave so she could come to New York when my ship arrived so we could have a few days together. She arranged it, and when the *U.S.S. General George O. Squier* docked, Millie was already ensconced at the Hotel Taft.

Our recreation officer had arranged a ship's party for that same evening at the Hotel Roosevelt, so I called Millie and told her we'd be going out that night. I picked her up in a taxi and we had a memorable evening of dancing, and, for me, a bit of an alcoholic beverage.

Until that night, in my entire life of 32 years, I had never seriously considered marriage. But after getting back to her hotel room, as we sat on her bed for a good-night smooch, it suddenly hit me: The war was over, and soon we'd be going our separate ways—she to Ohio and me to Virginia. We might never see each other again. Before I knew it, I was asking her to marry me.

She unwrapped herself from my embrace and called my attention to the fact that I wasn't exactly sober; but if I would come back the next day with the same proposal, she would give it her best consideration. No kidding.

Well, back I came the following afternoon—and this time she said yes. She called her mother and I called mine. When Mom asked me when we planned to wed, I said we wished we could do it right away, but didn't know how to go about it in New York. Then she reminded me that her brother, Capt. R. Duncan Gatewood, lived in New York and knew the city like a book. He might be able to help us.

I called him, and as I remember it, the conversation went like this:

"Uncle Dunc, this is Buddy."

"Buddy? Where are you?"

"Here in New York, and I want to get married."

"Right here?"

"Yes, and within the next few days."

"Do you want a church wedding or a civil ceremony?"

"A church wedding."

"OK, how about the Little Church Around the Corner?"

"That would be super, if you could do it."

"Consider it arranged. Will you have time for a honeymoon?"

"Maybe two days, but Millie will have to give up her hotel room on November 12." New York City was full of Armed Forces personnel coming and going, and the hotels limited stays to five days.

"So what's your timetable?" Uncle Dunc continued. "In New York you have to wait three days after getting a license before you can marry, unless you can get a justice of New York's Supreme Court to sign a waiver. You'll have to handle that yourself."

"OK, this is Friday. I'll get the license tomorrow morning and the waiver that same day, and we can be married on Monday. But what about the honeymoon? We don't have a place to stay."

"How about the Waldorf?"

"You couldn't really get us a room there, could you?"

"I'll take care of that, and arrange a champagne reception there right after the ceremony. I'll have a limousine."

Millie remembered a Navy friend from Florida who was also on leave and who lived in Mount Vernon, N.Y. She agreed to be maid of honor, and I had a few shipmates eager to attend, so a reception was just what was needed. Capt. Gatewood would be my best man. What an uncle!

But there was one more river to cross. We got the license all right, and a list of home addresses and phone numbers of the court justices who lived in the area. The trouble was, this was a long weekend, with Armistice Day falling on Sunday and the holiday on Monday, our wedding day. The justices might be away for the weekend. I started calling the names on the list, but got only one answer: a boy who, after some hesitation, told me the judge wasn't home.

Pretty downhearted by now, we had a quick lunch while we contemplated our next move. We came to the conclusion that our best bet was

We were told we had to wait three days after the wedding license was issued to get married, unless we got a justice of New York's Supreme Court to sign a waiver.

the boy who had told us his father wasn't home. Maybe Dad had told him to tell that to anyone who called—but if he *was* home, surely he wouldn't have the heart to turn away a couple of sailors on his doorstep who were waiting to get married.

We found a bus to take us to the judge's apartment, so we went there and pressed the button by his nameplate. Wouldn't you know it? The same boy answered the same way: Dad wasn't home.

I told the boy our story, and that we badly needed his father's help. Maybe if his father *was* home, he would let us in just long enough to sign a paper. Sure enough, Dad was home, and would be glad to help two members of the Armed Forces. He couldn't have been nicer. He asked us a few questions in a fatherly way, signed the waiver, and wished us well. Our guardian angels had been on the job!

Millie called her base in Florida to get her leave extended, and we were married on schedule. The two-day stay at the Waldorf Astoria was a dream. We danced Monday evening to Emil Coleman's orchestra, and on Tuesday my ship sailed for Calcutta. That was the last time we saw each other until early 1946.

On the way to Calcutta, the *Squier* stopped at Suez, beginning what was probably the second-greatest day of my life. Before traversing the canal, half the ship's company, including me, was taken by limousine to Gaza, where Egypt's pyramids stretched into the sky. The largest one was open to visitors, so I followed a bearded man with turban and white robe into a steep passageway that took us into the room where Cheops' mummy had lain. The only light was the stub of a candle held by the guide. It was a once-in-a-lifetime experience, but scary. I could hardly wait to get back into the sunlight.

Uncle Dunc died at age 91, which is my present age. Millie is a few years younger. My Uncle Dunc was a great man. He helped start something that has lasted nearly 60 years, producing four fine children. We will never forget his help in making Nov. 12, 1945, the greatest day of my life. ❖

Grandma's Big Kid

By Audrey Corn

We were living in Brooklyn, N.Y., in 1945 when the war ended. Church bells pealed, grown men embraced on the streets, and my normally dignified Grandpa grabbed Grandma and danced her out the kitchen door and onto their front porch.

I also remember Grandma's tears of joy a few months later when the Western Union telegram arrived. Uncle was back in the states and on his way home! Grandpa tipped the messenger boy the unheard-of sum of *50* cents!

Uncle had enlisted in the armed services straight out of high school. In fact, he missed the beginning of his own graduation party because he and some classmates stopped at the recruitment center to sign up.

Uncle had just turned 17.

Grandma and Grandpa were proud that their youngest child wanted to serve, but it nearly broke their hearts to see their baby go off to war. They mailed letters and care packages. And they prayed.

Grandpa bought war bonds and Grandma rolled bandages. And they prayed.

And now Uncle was home!

I'd never seen such hugging and kissing and carrying on in my entire 8 years. Finally Grandma dried her eyes and took a long, hard look at her youngest. "You're nothing but skin and bones," she mourned.

The relatives said Uncle looked lean and fit. Grandma ignored them. She cooked her baby's favorite foods and told him to eat everything on his plate or he wouldn't get any dessert.

Uncle didn't seem to mind the scolding and pampering. In fact, he acted like he enjoyed it! He winked at me and dutifully ate his green peas. Homework was even funnier. Grandma was very strict about homework. She called the GI Bill a precious gift. Each night, she cleared the kitchen table and ordered Uncle to sit down and do his homework so he could "make something of himself."

Uncle had a different agenda. College was an opportunity to be a boy again. Grandma lectured till she was blue in the face. It sounded like old times—a comfort to both of them.

The years passed. Uncle completed his college education under the GI Bill. Along the way, he finished growing up. He also met a pretty coed.

Uncle liked to tell people how he met his coed. He said he fell in love with her the minute he saw her in English 101. The course required a lot of reading, along with frequent trips to the college library. One day, Uncle followed his pretty coed when she left the library. She was listing badly to one side, so Uncle introduced himself and offered to carry her book bag.

The young lady had already noticed Uncle in her English class and she gratefully surrendered her satchel. "It's never felt this heavy before. I guess I borrowed too many books," she apologized.

Uncle and the coed got to talking. They boarded the subway train together. When the train pulled into her station, Uncle got off with her. He gallantly carried her book bag right up to her front door.

The young lady's mama heard their voices on the porch and invited Uncle in for an after-school snack. Later that night, Uncle's coed discovered that Uncle had snuck several heavy volumes of Greek history into her book bag. She wasn't studying Greek history.

By then, she had already agreed to a Saturday-night date. She decided to keep it.

The next thing we knew, Uncle and his sweetheart were making wedding plans. Grandma was delighted. She wanted her "baby" to be happy, get a good education, and marry a loving wife. Now Uncle had all three.

I owe some of my happiest postwar memories to Grandma and her big kid, and the love they shared back in the Good Old Days. ❖

My Sunshine Years

By Dorothy Carter Steiner

My boyfriend was with the Army Engineers in Europe and my daddy was on a Navy submarine in the Pacific. The best year of my life was 1946, when the clouds of fear and worry finally lifted with the safe return of those two.

During World War II, I was a teenager, and the apprehension and uncertainty of life were stressful. There were constant reminders of the reality of war. Year after year, the news had been all about the devastation taking place. At the movies, before the main film, a newsreel showed the horrors of war across the seas. Our only communication with servicemen was by mail. Letters I received were cut up and blanked out by the censors. And even while reading a letter, I did not know if my loved one was still alive.

The next year we were married. We had very few material things to begin with, but my husband had a car. He said he was never going to walk anywhere again.

Every day on the home front was strained and not much fun. Whole families moved away, taking our school chums with them. They went to work in defense factories. Even as I walked around town, there were reminders of the war. In the windows of some homes there hung flags with a gold star to indicate that a serviceman from that family had been killed.

In school, we were encouraged to bring our dimes to buy stamps to fill up our saver books, which we exchanged for war bonds. Ration books controlled the purchase of food, shoes and gasoline. Nobody had a spare tire—if, indeed, they had a car. There was no escape from the fact of war.

I graduated from high school in 1945. Later that year, I got a job at the F.W. Woolworth store in Bemidji, Minn. The years of making do or doing without were fading. Until now, we had brushed our teeth with tooth powder or baking soda shaken out into our hand. We had used water softener for shampoo, stood in line for a box of soap flakes, and, lacking silk stockings,

we girls smeared a brown liquid cosmetic on our legs to resemble stockings. Of course, if we were caught in the rain, our legs streaked.

Some merchandise was still scarce, but working in the store had its compensations. Clerks got first chance at a shipment of a dozen nylon stockings. Likewise, anything made of metal or rubber was slow to show up on store shelves.

My boyfriend and I were planning to be married, so I collected things for my "hope chest." Some girls had real cedar chests, but my hope chest was a cardboard box. At the store, I had first chance at a toaster, which cost me $1.98. It was the kind on which both sides turned down to receive the bread. It had to be watched closely or it burned up the bread, resulting in a smoky kitchen.

We were married at my mother's home. We had a two-tiered wedding cake from the bakery, and after the ceremony, Mother provided a meal for the relatives who crowded into the living room.

I bought basic kitchen tools. I embroidered pillowcases and dresser scarves and stashed everything away in my hope box. I got the first set of table flatware that showed up in a shipment at the store. The stock girl in the basement let me in on that find.

The next year we were married. We had very few material things to begin with, but my husband had a car. He said he was never going to walk anywhere again; he had had enough of that in the Army. I had $100 saved at the bank, squeezed out of my $17-a-week salary. That was our security. There was sunshine and we had faith and courage.

I spent the morning of our wedding setting my hair in pin curls and combing it out myself. I got all gussied up in a blue suit, a hat with a veil and high-heeled shoes, which I never wore again. I even had gloves and a new purse for going away. My husband wore a new dark suit. I had a big corsage and he had a rosebud boutonniere.

We were married at my mother's home. We had a two-tiered wedding cake from the bakery, and after the ceremony, Mother provided a meal for the relatives who crowded into the living

room. My husband purchased a box of cigars to give away to his men friends, and even offered one to the minister, who turned it down.

Sometime during the festivities, the men in the company were up to no good. We later found that they had tied tin cans to our car and festooned the whole thing with toilet tissue. Thus adorned, we drove 150 miles to Duluth, Minn., for our honeymoon.

We rented a little house. Houses were advertised as "modern" or "not modern"; if modern, they had water, sewer and an indoor bathroom. Our first home was "not modern" except for light bulbs hanging from the ceiling on cords.

My husband worked as a mechanic and we added to our belongings. We bought a bed and a kitchen table and chairs with tubular steel legs and a white kitchen cabinet. That cupboard was a free-standing piece of furniture. It had drawers and places for dishes and kettles and a pull-out work counter. Marvelous! It even had a flour bin with a built-in sifter.

Our money did not go far, so we raided the landlady's garden with her permission. Neighbors borrowed things back and forth, like flour, sugar and eggs. On payday, they were paid back.

Before long, we bought our first house. We had fun. We went to barn dances and friends came to play cards. We went fishing and had picnics. Company joined us for meals or just a cup of coffee.

A baby girl was born to us. She slept in a $12 buggy at home and in a dresser drawer at Grandma's house. A couple of years later she was joined by a baby brother. Our children grew into adulthood and they are my two favorite people. If circumstances had been different, and I had lost my future mate in the war, I would not have them.

I relive the thrill of that blessed beginning in 1946, when my hopes and prayers were at last answered and life resumed on a happier note. ❖

Yearbook Romance

By Audrey Carli

I wasn't even thinking about a husband-to-be when I flicked the pages of my friend's visitor's 1948 high-school yearbook. Sandra was from the neighboring Michigan town and had wanted to share the book during her weekend visit at Jane's home. So I scanned the pages until one senior boy's photo seemed to leap off the page at me. For some reason, his smile, thick-lashed eyes and wavy brown hair warmed my heart, and I sensed an immediate attraction. But surely it was impossible to become infatuated with a stranger's *picture*. … I dismissed the glow in my emotions.

After all, life was no fairy tale with a Prince Charming. I decided not to mention my feelings. Then I suddenly blurted, "Who is that?" in what I hoped was a nonchalant voice as I pointed to the photo.

"Oh, that's David Carli," the visitor said.

"Oh," I calmly replied. I kept flipping through the pages until I had looked at the entire book. But I said nothing about how David's picture tugged at my heart. It was too mysterious to explain!

Months flitted by and I gave no more thought to David or his photo. Then the following year, during football season, our school played David's, although he had graduated by then. There was a social gathering with music and dancing in our opponent's high school auditorium afterward and my friend Dorothy and I decided to attend. The crowded hall was filled with the music of recordings such as *Golden Earrings* and *The Old Lamplighter.*

I mingled with friends and discussed the game while Dorothy danced with her friend, Ron. I danced with a few friends, then sat down. Then Dorothy came over and said, "Keep sitting there. Don't dance with anyone else. Dave Carli is here. He wants to dance with you. Ron told me."

When Dave walked over to me, his blue eyes shimmering with friendliness, my heart again leaped—and I had no idea why! I had never seen the young man before in my life—except for his yearbook photo.

After we had danced to a couple of songs like *Near You* and *Till the End of Time*, Dave and I sat down. He reached into his pocket and showed me a photo of myself. "Where did you get that?" I gasped, stunned but pleasantly surprised.

"Someone we both know—but I won't say who, because he asked me not to—had two pictures of you. When I said I'd like one, he handed it to me. I can't explain it, but I wanted to meet you when I saw your picture!"

After that, Dave took to driving to my home from his neighboring town and visiting my family and me. We went to movies, family gatherings and school events. And finally, I admitted that I had been attracted to his picture.

We soon realized that we enjoyed the same kind of music and long, leisurely walks. We both had faith in God and looked forward to happy lives someday, no matter which pathway we took—together or apart. The magnetism between us grew into deep and permanent love during the three years that we dated. He was studying to become a teacher when we were married at the Church of Gesu on the Marquette University campus in Milwaukee on Feb. 2, 1952.

We had four children—three daughters, Debbie, Lynn and Lori, and one son, Glenn—during the first eight and a half years of marriage. Dave wrote me love letters throughout the years and I replied with letters of my own. Birthdays, anniversaries, holidays and ordinary days became reasons for our letters to each other. And they nourished our marriage and kept our love strong.

Although I wasn't thinking of a love interest when I looked at Sandra's high-school yearbook, I found my husband there! ❖

Our First Date

By Marjorie H. Benton

V alentine's Day has a very special meaning for me, because on that day in 1947, my boyfriend made our engagement official by slipping a diamond ring on my finger. Each year, Valentine's Day takes me back to our first date, a blind date, which turned out to be eye-opening.

Valentines Day in 1946, though, was pretty much a bust. I was 20 years old and had no boyfriend. There was no way I could know that this was the year I would graduate from college, get my first job *and* meet the man I was to marry.

Throughout the four years of college, we girls had lamented the lack of boys; most of them were in the service. In the words of a popular song of the time, "The best are in the Army, the rest will never harm me." For a while, some Air Force cadets were at the college taking special language courses, but this was a short interlude in the otherwise barren desert of our undergraduate years.

In the second semester of the 1945–1946 school year, however, a few veterans began filtering back to school. There was hope after all!

That spring, a friend on my floor announced that a very attractive and eligible fellow of her acquaintance had just returned home to her neighborhood, and she was going to get a date. After all, she boasted, she could get anyone she wanted, and he just had been discharged after more than a year overseas. Surely he would be easy prey for an enterprising young lady!

> *My date and I seemed to get along well enough, despite a lot of interference from the front seat, where my female "friend" kept turning around to direct her conversation at my date.*

In those days a girl couldn't just call up a man and ask for a date, so she made a plan. She had had an off-and-on relationship with the veteran's brother, and she was sure that he was still interested in her, so she decided to arrange a double date. She would date the brother and some girl of her choice would date the veteran. Thus she could flaunt her womanly wiles to the returning soldier and, she was certain, would soon be dating him.

She lost no time in talking with the brother, and he went for the bait. Step one of her plan was set up. Next, who was the lucky girl who would be the veteran's date?

As I lived within a reasonable distance of the unsuspecting young man's home, I was a likely candidate for "the other woman." She apparently did not think that I was any threat to her plan, and it apparently didn't occur to her that all might not go exactly as she expected. So it was arranged, and on a Saturday night we all took in a drive-in movie.

My date and I seemed to get along well enough, despite a lot of interference from the front seat, where my female "friend" kept turning around to direct her conversation at my date. When we parted for the night, no further plans were made, and after a few days I began to wonder. Maybe my friend was getting the date she had hoped for.

However, I was still interested—even though when my mother asked me about him, I answered, "He's OK, but I wouldn't want to marry him. He talks too much." Famous last words! Not ready to write him off,

I "coincidentally" showed up at a field one day where he was playing baseball. Between innings, he dropped over to talk with me, and before the last inning, we had a date for the next weekend.

From then on, things developed rapidly. We dated all the rest of the summer, with him wooing me with sweet pea bouquets from his mother's garden. Despite the fact that he locked the car keys in the car on our third date (which should have warned me that I was getting involved with an absent-minded man), we were still together when he was due to return to college and I was to start my new teaching job.

During the ensuing months of our separation, we wrote many letters back and forth and met on as many weekend visits as we could manage. During one of them, I sealed our fate by making him a cherry pie, my specialty and his favorite.

Our romance seemed to be flourishing, but it took some time for action to take place. It seemed to be up to me to make the next move.

My perfect opportunity came at the end of my first term of teaching, when I coyly asked him if I should sign my contract for the next year. "Well," he said, "I think we ought to be able to work out something better than that." Before the end of that evening, we were unofficially—but definitely—engaged.

On Valentine's Day, the deal was sealed with the purchase of an engagement ring. We were married the following August, and for the past 57 years, it has been my tradition to make him a cherry pie on Valentine's Day.

And there was an added bonus: We've had a lot of chuckles about the way my friend's plan backfired. ❖

Takin' a Chance On Love

By Elizabeth Bowman Good

During World War II, if you recall, civilians were encouraged to write to our people in the service to help keep up their morale. I wrote to a few young men—nothing serious, just everyday news about "action on the home front" as we prayed with them that the war would end soon and successfully.

While my sister Ruth's husband, Thad, was on a ship in the Pacific, she lived in San Diego, Calif., next-door to the Tweed family. My sister and Gayle Tweed became close friends. Upon learning that Ruth had a sister in high school and Gayle a brother in the Air Force, they dreamed up the idea that it would be nice if these two wrote to one another. Gale gave my sister a picture of Sie to send to me and Ruth gave her one of me to send to Sie. Having done their duty, they left the rest to us and fate.

Sie and I were receptive to the notion and we wrote to one another for the rest of the war. We sent pictures back and forth and shared our hopes and dreams for when our world would be at peace again. I didn't make any concrete plans for the two of us, but Sie was thinking of the kind of wife he would need. He hoped to rent his parents' farm and their dairy cows, and he needed a farm girl who would be content to stay home rather than gadding about too much. She would know how to milk cows, keep a neat house, cook, garden, can and help on the farm in a pinch. And, as they would be starting out on a shoestring, she would need to know how to stick to a budget.

It occurred to Sie that his Arkie girl might just be the kind of wife he was looking for. He wanted to hang onto her, at least until he learned for himself if she was for real.

When he learned that my parents were about the same age as his own and that I was the youngest in a family of 10 living brothers and sisters and aunt to a host of nieces and nephews, the picture grew even brighter, as his parents were raising two granddaughters, ages 5 and 3.

I had never even seen an electric milking machine; the TVA's plans to electrify our part of the country were interrupted abruptly when the war effort snapped up all the copper. We still hand-milked our cows. Our home was illuminated by coal-oil lamps and we burned wood for

heating and cooking. And on laundry day we did our wash with the big old three-legged iron wash pot, galvanized tubs, a scrub board, bars of P&G laundry soap, a can of lye, a bottle of Mrs. Stewart's bluing, a box of Argo starch and lots of elbow grease, just as we'd always done. We didn't miss modern conveniences because we'd never had them.

It occurred to Sie that his Arkie girl might just be the kind of wife he was looking for. He wanted to hang onto her, at least until he learned for himself if she was for real. But it crossed his mind that there could be some fickleness involved, so he was cautious about it. He asked that I use the money he sent to buy a ring—not an engagement ring, but just a small diamond promise one, meaning only that I would not marry another until the two of us had a chance to meet. I had no serious boyfriend on the string and I was as curious as Sie was, so I bought a dainty little diamond ring for $75 when I was visiting one of my other sisters in Dallas.

Sie was discharged in the fall of 1945. He went deer hunting with a cousin. Then he got his bright royal blue 1930 Model-A Ford in apple-pie order and headed for Arkansas. He arrived at our house on the cold morning of Dec. 1. I met him at the door with a hug and a kiss.

Mama gave him a warm, friendly smile. But my father had plastered a distrustful scowl all over his face. He only grunted a chilly hello before starting his inquisition. In the first place, he was opposed to having his daughter go so far from home, especially with a former soldier whom he'd never met before. He came close to laying Sie on the floor and walking all over his face. "How do I know you are what you profess to be? For all I know, you could have a wife already up there in Washington—and children!"

Daddy's attitude was downright embarrassing, but Sie had come well prepared. He laid out his life's history on the dining room table for my father's inspection.

We chose the shortest route we could take from Arkansas to Washington. Since we hadn't much money, we decided to conserve by sleeping every other night in the Model A.

Mama wasn't as suspicious, distrusting person. I had shared portions of Sie's letters with her. She took one look at his honest face and the expression on my own and added another son to her brood.

Sie proposed to me on Dec. 2 and Brother Wilson married us in Marianna on the 11th, my 20th birthday, with only my brother David and his wife, Mildred, in attendance. We spent our very brief honeymoon—one night—in Memphis, where we went to the movies and saw *Wuthering Heights* and stayed at the King Cotton Hotel. We returned to Moro the following day, packed my things and left for Washington on the 13th.

We chose the shortest route we could take from Arkansas to Washington. Since we hadn't much money, we decided to conserve by sleeping every other night in the Model A. So on the night of the 13th, Sie pulled the car off into an open field. We ate our supper of dry crackers washed down with cold milk. Then he made me a bed by removing the backseat of the car and putting it lengthwise across the backs of both seats. He wadded himself up in the front seat and was soon snoring away.

I was still wide awake and half-frozen by 4 a.m., so I woke him up and "generously" gave him my bed. I shivered until it got light outside. Then the bride woke the groom, and when we looked outside, we saw that every limb, twig and blade of grass was solidly encased in ice!

The car was sluggish about starting—its innards were as cold as my own—but after a lot of coaxing, we got it to take us to the closest city so we could wash up. The closest place we found open was the courthouse, but the ladies' room was locked up tight, so my beloved told me he would stand guard while I used the men's.

I should have known right then that I would be basically responsible for myself from here on out, for when I came out of my little cubicle, I was face to face with a strange man! I don't recall whether there was a light on, but it wasn't needed. My face gave off enough illumination! I didn't stay to wash my face or brush my teeth. Once outside the room, I found my husband sitting in a chair down the hall, placidly reading a newspaper.

Our second night found us in Dodge City, Kan. After we ate a warm supper, we slept like logs in a very comfortable bed. It was wonderful to be warm, but that lasted only until the next morning. We woke to 13 degrees below zero, and faced a radiator that was frozen solid, including the antifreeze. When we finally got the car going to the nearest service station, Sie had to hang his head out the window to see beyond the steam boiling up from the radiator.

The heater had gasped its last during the freeze-up, so we traveled the rest of the way bundled in coats, blankets and gloves. The route we had chosen had many, many roads that were mountainous sheets of ice, so we did our share of skidding.

Needless to say, we didn't sleep in the car any more after that first night. We figured that any money we saved would be useless if we were a couple of frozen corpses!

With gratitude to God, we arrived in Seattle on Christmas Eve and were invited to spend the evening with friends of Sie's. On Christmas Day, we came on to Mount Vernon, where I met Sie's two brothers, the wife and children of one, and the other whose little girls Sie's parents were raising. They were beautiful children who were to fill the vacancy in my heart left by my nieces and nephew back in Arkansas.

With the help of Sie's brother, we fixed up a tiny house called "the Shack"—and it looked like it on the outside. But inside it was like a doll's house, with a living room, bedroom, kitchen, tiny dinette, hallway and bathroom. I could stand in the middle of any room and hit

The heater had gasped its last during the freeze-up, so we traveled the rest of the way bundled in coats, blankets and gloves. Needless to say, we didn't sleep in the car any more after that first night.

all its corners with the dust mop. With 16 people in the place, there was sitting room only if they sat in every room, including the bathroom.

The Shack was situated between Dry Slough and Dry Slough Road. The slough was fed twice daily by the tides coming in from Skagit Bay. I don't know how deep the water was at high tide, but when it was out, it was 10 feet deep at the end of the bridge we had to cross to get to the farm.

We lived very close to Sie's parents, and his mother became my dearest friend. She adored our four children as much as they did her. She and I went places together, and when I was planning to go to town, I'd phone her and ask if she wanted to go. Nine chances in ten, her reply was, "Just wait until I get my apron off and my coat on."

Busy Dry Slough Road was frequented by all the farmers. The Shack was separated from the road only by a very short bridge, extending from our small porch to the three steps going down the side of the dike. As we were so close to the busy road, Mom had to keep a constant lookout for the children's safety.

We were blessed to have her nearby for 26 years; only twice did the two of us have a disagreement, and those were over things too minor to mention.

My father-in-law was noted for having a bad temper. I saw him display it a few times. If he got very angry with someone, he might not speak to him for as long as three years. Still, when he became ill and needed love and care, he was just another of my babies until his death.

Sie and I have been married for more than 55 years at the time of this writing, and well over half of them have been very happy. Though we haven't lived on a bed of thornless roses, our life has been a pleasant one for the most part, and we feel the Lord blessed us by giving us the opportunity of takin' a chance on love. ❖

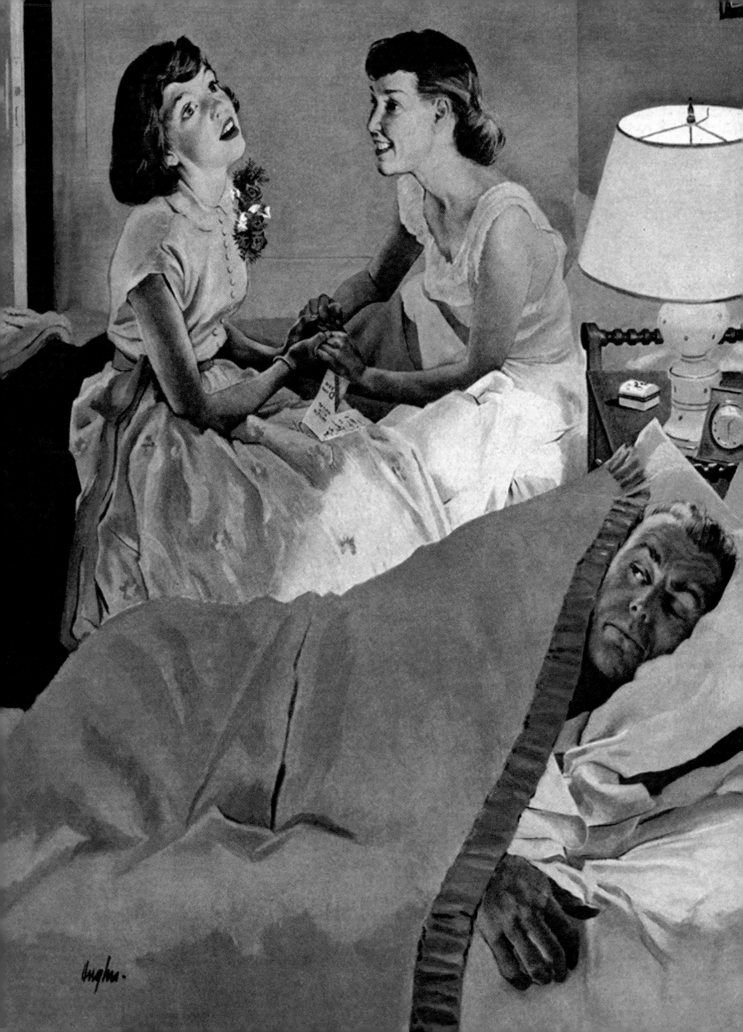

Moments to Remember

By Loise Pinkerton Fritz

*I*t was V-E Day. World War II had ended and the country was basking in victory. "Johnnies" were marching home to tickertape parades, ringing church bells, "welcome home" hugs and kisses and other festivities, all honoring and thanking those who so honorably served our country. It was a great day for the United States!

Although it was a jubilant time, it was also a bittersweet time. Many families and friends enjoyed the sweet taste of reunion, but for those whose loved ones had given their all on foreign soil for our country's freedom, there was a bitter side, a touch of sadness. Still, beneath that sadness lay pride in the hearts of those who realized what their sons and daughters had done to keep our country free.

But let me get back to the "Johnnies" who came marching home. Among them was my "Johnnie." Delbert was his name. And I would have to say that he came sailing home, for after high-school graduation, he enlisted in the Navy. While he was still stationed in the United States, he'd come to see me when he was on leave. Often he'd "thumb" his way home when he had only a weekend leave.

It was during one of these visits that he revealed that he had had his eye on me when we both rode the big yellow school bus from our valley to the "big" high school in town. However, since he was younger than I was, I hadn't really paid attention to him. It was during our high-school years that my brother suggested he ask me for a date. That's when our romance began.

When he came home on leave, we went square-dancing, bicycling, hiking and horseback-riding. Sometimes we just strolled down country lanes hand-in-hand. We also went to outdoor movies and attended hayrides. In winter, we went skiing, ice-skating and sleigh-riding.

We were pros at none of these, but we had lots of fun.

In the summer we went fishing. On one of these occasions, it caused quite a stir when I kept reeling in the fish while they seemed to evade his bait. He was the fisherman, but when we went fishing together, I'd make the catch.

When he was home on leave on a Sunday, we attended his church where he was a member and I was the organist.

He often asked me to marry him, but I could never make up my mind to leave home. I had such good parents and such a wonderful home life that it was difficult for me to leave. However, I was sure he'd be a good husband. In the meantime, he just waited, bent on winning my hand.

One night when he was home on leave, we went to a church picnic in the church grove. There he gave me an engagement ring. When I asked Mother if I could accept it, she nodded in the affirmative. Seven years later we were married in my home church in the country. The minister who performed the ceremony and his wife, who was the witness, were the only two at the wedding. After a one-day honeymoon, I got homesick and Delbert had to bring me home!

Upon our return, we immediately moved into our new home that he had built, just a field away from my parents. To this day, he tells everyone that this was the farthest he could get me from my childhood home and parents.

We've been married more than 50 years now, and the Lord has showered us with many blessings. Though we were not blessed with children, I believe the Lord had other plans for us. He gave me the gifts of music and writing and my husband the knowledge to supervise the building of hospitals, nursing homes, schools and homes like the one he built us.

I remember an old song that says, "There's a lid for every pot." Our marriage has proved that! ❖

The Five-Cylinder Nash

By William R. Reading

During World War II, I enlisted in the Navy. The year was 1943 and for the first two years, I was stationed in Newfoundland, serving on the YO-65, a small yard oiler. We delivered fuel to stations all along the coast.

My next duty was in New London, Conn., at the submarine base. From New London I could get home to Flemington, N.J., on weekend liberty, and I went home every chance I got. It was great to visit my family and friends after being away from home for two years.

Eventually I took my 1927 Nash back to New London with me, traveling the Merrit Parkway and then the Old Post Road to the base. The car made many trips back and forth, and many times there was a load of sailors with me. I would drop them off in New York City and pick them up again on my return.

I had bought the car from a neighbor, an 85-year-old lady by the name of Mary Gray. She was quite a lady, a one-room schoolteacher for many years, and then the first woman secretary in Flemington. The town fathers had quietly asked her to stop driving, and that is how I became the proud owner of her 1927 Nash sedan. It cost me $75, all I could afford with my small salary at the A&P store in town.

My father told me there was a 1927 Nash sedan for sale. It was not exactly what I had in mind, but it was in good shape and mileage was low.

My father, a mechanic, had told me that she might be willing to sell it. As it was a sedan, it was not exactly what I had in mind, but it was in good shape and the mileage was low—only 18,000 miles. It had curtains in the back windows and, with my gas ration "A" sticker, it buzzed me around until I enlisted.

I finally received my discharge on April Fool's Day 1946. I planned to get married in June, when my wife-to-be would be graduating from Flemington High School, and I was trying to find a good job.

But jobs were very hard to find, as so many servicemen were home looking, too, and the country was busy changing over from war production to peacetime industry. I did manage to get a temporary job helping out on my cousin's farm.

We were married the day after my fiancée graduated from high school. Neither of us had any savings, but we did have lots of optimism and determination. So once we were married, we took off in my old Nash "Susabella" with a tank full of gas, three quarts of used motor oil and $40, and headed for the beautiful Pocono Mountains.

We spent our first night at a roadside cabin. The elderly landlady was something of a fortune-teller. The next morning, after reading our palms, she predicted that we would have a long and happy marriage.

On the spur of the moment, I decided to take my wife to New London to show her where I had spent my time in the Navy when I was not at home seeing her. As we went through the tollbooth heading north on the Merrit Parkway, the tollbooth operator said that it had been quite awhile since he had seen me. (It paid to have a fancy car that was different from what most people had.)

All too soon our money ran low and so we headed back to New Jersey. Old Susabella was running pretty well, but she leaked a little engine oil as we cruised along, and I failed to keep the oil level up to par. While pushing the throttle a little too hard, I heard a loud clatter. I soon realized what the problem was: A con-

Eleanor and me on our wedding day in June 1946, sitting atop Susabella, my 1927 Nash.

necting rod bearing had knocked out. I pulled off onto the grass shoulder and sat, wondering how we would ever get home.

Finally, I remembered my Dad mentioning that my car was one of the few in which the piston and rod could be removed from the bottom of the crankcase. It was a six-cylinder, so I reasoned that I could still drive on five cylinders.

I had some tools with me, so I crawled under the car, took out about 30 bolts and dropped the pan. Removing the bad bearing and piston, I jammed a rag up in the top of that cylinder to keep the oil from splashing out. I then put the pan, with some oil still in it, back in place—no easy job. After I cranked the starter for quite a while, she finally started up. She sounded like a two-cylinder Maxwell, but with God watching over

my shoulder, we somehow made it—slowly—back to Flemington.

That was more than 50 years ago. Can you imagine doing that today along the parkway?

Susabella has long since gone to that great junkyard in the sky. We have many fond memories of that first car of mine—like the time the fan blade went through the radiator, or the time I put oversized tires over undersized tubes. But those are other stories.

With three children, five grandchildren and one great-granddaughter, we still enjoy the long and happy marriage that the fortune-teller forecasted for us. And we are still traveling, only now with our truck and trailer. Exploring the beauties of this lovely country of ours is one of the things we love most. ❖

A Night of Destiny

By Frederick M. Smith

The sky was a chalice, overflowing with sparkling, bubbling, brilliant stars. Looking at it, we knew something special was going to happen that night. Five of us, all newly graduated sailors stationed at Bainbridge Naval Training Center, were in Baltimore on liberty, doing what we presumed sailors were supposed to do. Suddenly we saw an advertisement for a "moonlight cruise" that was scheduled to sail that very evening.

After a short discussion, we unanimously decided to spend the evening at sea—or at least on Baltimore's harbor and upper Chesapeake Bay. "After all," we said to each other, "we can drink a little beer, do some dancing, and, if we're lucky, add some solace to the lives of some lonely young women."

The evening progressed and we did indeed drink some beer, until we arrived at the point where we had enough courage to approach the ladies in search of dancing partners. This was 1951; I was only 20 years old. My buddies ranged in age from 20–23. We were a sorry selection of shy sailors, most of us away from home for the first time.

At one point during the evening, the orchestra was playing a Latin tune. We saw an attractive young lady crossing the dance floor and looking in our direction. Being the strong macho sailors that we were, we said to ourselves and to each other, "I hope she doesn't ask me to dance! I don't know how to rumba, or tango, or samba, or whatever it is they're playing!"

But the lady walked right up to one of us—naturally, the one who looked like a Nordic god—and said, "My girlfriend would like to dance with you."

This blond, handsome sailor, all six feet two inches of him, began to stammer and scuff his feet. Looking at the floor, he finally admitted, "I don't know how to dance to that song."

The rest of us, apparently feeling that men of the U.S. Navy shouldn't be so wimpy, asked, "Where is she? Which girl is it?"

We were duly introduced, and even though I could tell she was disappointed because she would not be dancing with the Nordic god, Rosemarie agreed to dance with me. I was told the orchestra was playing a rumba, and after a few instructions from my partner, we did a fairly creditable job. During the evening we danced several more times, and I finally asked her to go out on the deck with me.

Talking together under a canopy of stars, with the soft music in the background, we became attracted to each other.

Talking together under a canopy of stars, with the soft music in the background, we became attracted to each other. Her hair was raven, dark and shining in the moonlight. As we talked, I gently touched it to prove to myself that it was as soft as it looked. It was.

Finally I worked up enough nerve to ask if I could take her home. She hemmed and hawed but ultimately assented, with one condition: Patricia, the one who introduced us, had to go, too. They had come together, and by golly, they would leave together. Remember, this was 1951; it was a different world then.

I asked one of my buddies if he would go along to complete the party and he agreed. We drove my Rosemarie home first (I say "my" for I already felt in my heart that we would belong to each other). The four of us sat there on the porch, talking, before we said good night. And that's what we did: We *said* good night. No hugs, no kisses, just "Good night, it's been fun."

I did manage to ask her for a date and she accepted. Then my friend and I took the other girl, Pat, home and went back to Bainbridge Naval Center.

It was a week before I saw Rosemarie again. All I could think about during that week was *Rosemarie*, *Rosemarie*. Each day I said her name out loud, just to see how it sounded.

Finally the big day arrived: I was going on my first date with my girl. (I had already written to my family in Swissvale, Pa., and told them I had met the girl I was going to marry. Talk about self-confidence!)

Rose met me at the front door. We went into the house and she introduced me to her family as "Frank." I thought, *I certainly did impress her; she can't even remember my name!* But I

was too shy to correct her in front of everybody.

Later, when I told her of her mistake, she was concerned. I said she could correct the error before I saw her again—which I thought was a clever way of setting up another date. I think it was *that* date that I was allowed to kiss her on the cheek.

We dated for a little less than two years and then, on Valentine's Day 1953, she became my wife. On Feb. 14, 2003, we celebrated 50 wonderful years of marriage. We have two marvelous children and four beautiful grandchildren.

I often wonder what became of that Nordic god who turned down the opportunity to dance a rumba with the raven-haired stranger. I'm eternally grateful for his shyness. ❖

I Married a War Veteran

By LaVonne M. Sparkman

My husband, Elmer Jay Sparkman, enlisted in the Army in February 1942, knowing that he would have been drafted as a single man at 21 years of age. He chose the Army because he would be stationed near his little hometown of Mineral, Wash., in western Washington state. Given a choice, he joined the signal corps at McChord Field, and served until December 1945.

Elmer had been driving a school bus 13 miles from Mineral to Morton, about 85 miles south of Seattle, and during school hours, he worked at a service station.

We met after my parents moved to Morton in 1948. Home from college, I took our car to the service station for gas, and the tall, handsome fellow with a wonderful smile waited on me. As so many World War II veterans married soon after the war, I assumed that he was not available. It was the next year before I learned that he was still single. Had it not been for the war, Elmer probably would have married sooner, but he didn't want to leave a wife while he was in the service. When we met, he was 30 years old and I was 20.

In the meantime, I was in college and became engaged to a young veteran I met there. I broke the engagement when Elmer and I started dating in the summer of 1949. A girlfriend who had known Elmer for many years got us together. She wanted to double-date with a fellow I had known since childhood and to whom I had introduced her.

One of our first dates was a 6-mile hike to a lake. We enjoyed each other's company so much that we began seeing each other frequently. My friends married in 1950.

The next day we began our honeymoon by driving down to Reno. At that time, because many women went to Reno to get a quick divorce, we thought it was fun to go there on our honeymoon instead.

Elmer proposed while I was in college, in the fall of 1949. We began making wedding plans. It had to be a simple wedding because my parents had recently built a nursing home and had a big debt. Elmer took me to Tacoma to buy a wedding dress, despite the custom of the groom not seeing the dress ahead of time.

We were married on Christmas Day in 1949. Why Christmas? Being a school bus driver, Elmer had time off during the holidays, and my maid of honor was on vacation from college. We asked the minister who had baptized me to officiate because I wanted to be married in his church. The only problem was that he usually read a very short ceremony, but I wanted to use vows that I had written. His made his only mistake when he asked me to take Elmer to be my lawfully wedded wife, but he quickly corrected it.

Christmas came on a Sunday that year, and the pastor would not dismiss his regular Sunday-evening church service, so our wedding didn't begin until 9 p.m. Being young, we didn't realize that attending a wedding on Christmas night would not be our guests' favorite activity after a full day.

Elmer did not want his new car decorated, so he hid it in the minister's garage. The next day we began our honeymoon by driving down the Oregon coast and on to San Francisco and Reno. At that time, because many women went to Reno to get a quick divorce, we thought it was fun to go there on our honeymoon instead.

During the 1940s, there was talk about "trial marriage." We joked that we would try our marriage for 60 years and then decide if we wanted to make it last. On Christmas 2003, we celebrated our 54th anniversary—which means six years to go! ❖

My Son's Wedding

By Edna Staples

Just before the war was over, my son Lynn enlisted for four years in the Air Force. He wasn't too happy to be tied up for four years, but he wanted a college education and could not afford it otherwise. He soon found out that the Air Force was a good place to be. He made friends and learned all about flight simulators, which he found very interesting.

Finally he was ready for the end of his enlistment. He had met a girl at a USO dance, and they were to marry as soon as he was mustered out. He had bought a Cessna 120 airplane and received his pilot's license. He even had gotten in a few college hours along with his simulator training, and had a job waiting for him with Link Aviation in Binghamton, N.Y.

Of course, we were very proud of him. He seemed to be successful at everything he undertook. When he brought his bride-to-be home, we all agreed he had made a good choice.

They invited us to the wedding in Nebraska, and I was delighted at the thought of going. My husband said he would stay home and take care of the business. We had a store and campground, and he felt he could not leave.

I had never traveled, but my younger son and his wife and child planned to go with me. I guess we were real hillbillies in those days, for I had never been anywhere.

When the wedding day arrived, we were there, excited by all the preparations. I had my new $9.98 dress from Sears. Dorothy, my daughter-in-law, had had her mother make her a white formal, as she was going to sing at the wedding. My youngest son, Danny, actually planned to wear a suit, and we had my little granddaughter fixed up like a little doll.

I watched the wonderful marriage ceremony with a lump in my throat. Was I losing my son or gaining a daughter?

I was passing the bride's room when I heard a bridesmaid say, "'Something old' … her mother's necklace. The 'something new' is her engagement ring. What will we do for 'something borrowed' and 'something blue'?"

"She can wear my garters; they'll be borrowed and they are blue," said the bridesmaid.

The wedding was very beautiful. The bride was lovely, and my son was handsome. Dorothy did not wear her white formal after all. The bride's mother said, "No one wears white in the wedding party except the bride," so she lent Dorothy a beautiful yellow formal.

I probably broke another rule, as I refused to leave my grandchild with a baby sitter. As the usher led me to my front-row seat, I was leading a small child by the hand as she called out, "Sing *Mary Had a Widdle Wamb,* Mommy!"

I watched the wonderful marriage ceremony with a lump in my throat. Was I losing my son or gaining a daughter?

The ceremony was soon over, the rice was thrown and the pictures taken. The young couple escaped to the high-school gym, where a bountiful dinner (I would say "supper") was served. I sat at the head table with the wedding party, nervous because I did not know which fork to use.

After the dinner, the bride excused herself and everyone was hugging and laughing. Under a hail of rice, the bride and groom escaped to the airport. Somewhere, somehow, the bride had changed from her long white dress into a navy blue suit. We watched the young couple climb into the Cessna 120, taxi down the short runway, and head for a blue patch of sky. It was getting a little cloudy as we stood, with our mouths open, looking up until the plane became a little speck.

As I hugged the bride's mother, I said, "I *have* gained a daughter." She responded, "And I have gained a *son*." ❖

How I Met My Wife

By John F. Maguire Jr.

*I*n December 1944, when I was medically discharged from the U.S. Army at Cushing General Hospital in Framingham, Mass., I returned to my family in nearby Arlington. As I tried to resume my life, I was faced with the task of adjusting to a completely different lifestyle than I had been living the previous two and one-half years.

I found this particularly troubling; the war was still going on and here I was, back in civilian life. I couldn't rid myself of feelings of guilt, and as the days wore on, I became increasingly miserable. I decided I had to get a job.

I started to look for work after the holidays. After much searching, I finally interviewed for a position with Stone & Webster Corporation in Boston. They had an opening in their blueprint room, a small, single-person office adjoining their regular business office. My duties were simple: to manage and maintain the small office and check out blueprints to company engineers as required. I would be working by myself and accountable to no one else. I could work in quiet and solitude. It was just what I was looking for.

As the game progressed, the three girls stood in a group not far from where I was. My father and the girls struck up a conversation. I learned afterward that he had told them all about me.

One day, a few months after I had settled into the job, an attractive young girl passed through the business office in the company of one of the engineers. I was immediately impressed by her outgoing, vivacious personality. She was full of life and she appealed to me instantly. But I saw her only for a moment, and then she was gone. I was shy and withdrawn back then, and I dismissed the incident from my mind. But I did learn that her name was Mary Davis.

During my tenure with Stone & Webster, I came to know Gerard Magner, who worked in the basement supply room. We became friendly and I learned that he managed the company baseball team. When he asked if I was interested in playing, I told him I was and joined up.

We played our games after work, taking public transportation to locations around Boston. It was fun. I played third base.

One spring evening we were scheduled to play at a field in the Fenway area. It was a well-maintained facility with cement stands along the third-base line. We arrived at the field and after warming up, we were all set to start. My father had come to watch. Gerard had been going with a girl named Clare Metzler. She also had come to see the game and had brought two girlfriends with her.

When I caught sight of them approaching the field, my heart jumped—there was Mary Davis again! She was one of Clare's girlfriends, and she was walking across the diamond to the stands in her high heels. I think I probably kept one eye on Mary for the rest of the evening.

As the game progressed, the three girls stood in a group not far from where I was. My father and the girls struck up a conversation. I learned afterward that he had told them all about me.

When the game ended, we all went our separate ways. My father gave me a ride home to Arlington. I never got to meet Mary that evening. But from that point on, I was definitely interested. Ironically, my father had gotten to meet and speak with my future wife before I even met her.

A day or so later, I saw Gerard and inquired about Mary. He asked me if I would be interested in going out on a date with her and said he would inquire through his girlfriend, Clare. Subsequently, a double date was arranged. We would go dancing that next Saturday night at the Totem Pole in Newton, where one of the Big Bands would be playing.

Saturday evening came. I finally got to meet Mary, and I was not disappointed. She turned out to be everything I thought she would be—charming, delightful and full of conversation the entire evening. She told me about her family—her brothers, who were in the service in different parts of the world; her father, a World War I hero who had passed away the previous year—and so many other interesting things.

I was hooked after the first date. We went together for about nine months and married in January 1946.

At the time of this writing, 56 years and five beautiful children later, we continue on with our lives, somewhat slower-paced but every bit as much in love as ever. Life has been good to us. ❖

Coral Sea

By Donald W. Lang

The sounds of a radio news report were drifting out of the first sergeant's tent as I ambled down the company street to look at the bulletin board. I paid little attention to it, but two words, "Coral Sea," did get through.

On the bulletin board there was a notice that our division would send seven soldiers to Officers Candidate School at Aberdeen Proving Ground in Maryland. Soon I was standing before the selection board, struggling to find answers to many questions. Finally, one captain asked, "What major battle is going on right at the moment?"

"The Battle of Coral Sea, sir," I blurted. It was a decisive answer, and my life changed forever right then and there.

Three months later I was the proudest soldier in the U.S. Army when two other brand-new second lieutenants and I strode into the Officers Club at Fort Story, Va. There we saw four Army nurses, standing with their backs to the bar, looking us over.

My pride vanished instantly. I had never seen a nurse before and didn't know how to act. Nonchalantly, we all picked up cue sticks and pretended to shoot pool. I did think the nurse on the end was kinda cute.

The next day, an older officer asked me if I would like a blind date with a nurse. I replied with a hearty "Yes!" Sure enough, when I knocked on the door of the nurses' quarters that evening, the cute little girl on the end answered and informed me that she was my date. Her name was Judy Pierce.

That blind date led eventually to a proposal of marriage. Eight months later I stood before the altar in the post chapel at Fort Story, my ego inflated as never before, as Col. George B. West escorted my bride down the aisle.

That was 60 years ago. We are still married and have a bright future. ❖

JOHN FALTER

Life After the Wedding Vows

By Helen Bolterman

Wedding bells rang for my husband, Wes, and me on April 2, 1949. We were married at the First Congregational Church in LaCrosse, Wis., at 4 p.m. that afternoon. It was a bright spring day and the sunbeams shone brightly in a beautiful array of colors through the lovely stained glass windows as I walked down the aisle on the arm of my proud father, to be wed to the love of my life.

A wedding reception for our guests was scheduled at my parents' home following the ceremony. Wes and I contributed financially to our wedding and reception, and we decided we could forgo renting a reception hall to save the $50 fee. My parents agreed to have it at their home. Mother, her friend and I baked several hams ahead of time and prepared the side dishes to make a delightful dinner for all those attending. Mother's friends Martha and Laura helped with the main course and Wes' sister Florence served coffee for our guests.

After all were served, the guests gathered in our living room and dining area for the gift opening. It was customary then for the bride and groom to open their wedding gifts together and display them for all to see. There were bath towel sets, sheets, cake plates, many relish dishes, a coffee pot, a favorite picture of ours of Jesus on the Mount from Wes' Aunt Fern, a warm wool blanket from my families' salesman friend Chris, and stemware and tableware from my bridesmaids. Employees from where Wes and I worked contributed to a gift of an electric mixer. No more mixing cakes with a wooden spoon! It even had an attachment for squeezing oranges for juice.

Wes and I mingled briefly with our guests before

we bid our farewells. Due to the late hour, we spent our wedding night at our rented apartment. The following morning, we boarded the train for a two-day honeymoon in Milwaukee.

We had made reservations at the Schroder Hotel for our stay in Milwaukee. Our first day we spent shopping close to the hotel. We ate dinner at a Chinese restaurant, which also served American fare that Wes preferred. That evening the hotel sponsored the Jan Garber orchestra. Wes and I decided our budget could handle the $4 admission to the dance, plus a glass each of the hotel's wine special. We sipped the wine sparingly as we enjoyed several dance numbers before retiring to our room for the night. The following day, we enjoyed dinner at an Italian restaurant and then retired early since we would be leaving the following morning for home.

On our arrival home, I tenderly tucked away my special ivory satin wedding dress in the Lane cedar chest that Wes and I had purchased as our engagement present for $50. As was customary for that time, I had stored in it embroidered dish towels, dollies and pillowcases, etc., that I had made or received as gifts.

Beginning housekeeping in our small apartment, Wes and I budgeted our money carefully. Prior to our wedding, we had purchased our living room set, a davenport and matching upholstered chair; a maple dining-room table and four chairs; our bedroom set consisting of bed, chest of drawers and a vanity with a mirror; an apartment-size gas stove and a refrigerator.

We purchased a secondhand Maytag washer for $15, bought several washtubs, and borrowed Wes' mother's copper boiler for heating wash water. My parents gave us an old kitchen table they had stored in their basement, which we could use until we could afford one of our own. We had few appliances, though Wes' mother had given us an old toaster that consisted of two heating elements on each side. The bread would be toasted on one side; then we would flip the bread to toast the other side.

One of my first salesmen callers was the coffee man who sold coffee, spices, vanilla, etc. The beauty of purchasing his wares was that

I could earn points for various premiums. My points gave me a 2-cup drip coffeemaker, a two-piece pan cover, and cookie sheets (which I still have 54 years later), plus other miscellaneous items. During his visits, I also gained insights such as advice on treating my sinus condition by eating garlic, purchasing the best spices or laundry soap, and, at times, a weather forecast.

Our cooking utensils were lean, too, in those early days. Then another salesman came to our rescue. If we would let him demonstrate his Wearever pans and cookware, we could invite several couples and he would cook us all a free dinner. It sounded good, although Wes was not that pleased with the idea. He was of the opinion that we could wait before buying additional cookware, but he finally gave his permission.

The salesman demonstrated how to cook with little water to save vitamins, especially when cooking our vegetables. The meal was delicious! I was sold, and purchased the whole set of Wearever. By doing so, I earned premiums for an aluminum pie plate, a colander and a heavy 8-quart soup kettle. We even had the option of paying for our Wearever over six monthly payments. We *still* are using this cookware, and Wes says, "It was the best investment we have ever made."

Over the years, as times prospered after the war, we added an automatic toaster, our own hot-water heater and automatic washer/dryer. After purchasing our home in 1954, we bought our first television set, a black-and-white model. Today our house is loaded with all the appliances available to make life comfortable and tasks easier—everything from a waffle maker, microwave, and automatic dishwasher to an automatic coffee maker, color television, and my precious computer.

And I no longer need to stand by the washing machine as I did in the 1940s and early 1950s, wringing each item of clothing by hand through the wash wringer, then rinsing everything in two washtubs and hanging them outside on a clothesline to dry in all kinds of weather. I now have the convenience of tossing my wash into our automatic dryer when the clouds predict rain. With all of these modern conveniences, we continue to enjoy the best years of our lives! ❖

Romance in the Arctic

By Alice Osborne

Romance! According to song, it happens often in strange, far-away places. Mine happened in Nome, Alaska. It was 1942 and there was a war underway. Over a casserole container I met *him*!

My friend Dorothy and I were bent low under a counter in Old Man Polet's store in a vain search for a glass oven dish when this large blond fellow swooped in to help. "Sorry. Next boat," he advised. We heard that a lot over winter. It was early November, the shelves were emptying, and the next boat wouldn't make it through the ice-choked Bering Sea until June.

Dorothy and I were wide-eyed new teachers in the "Far North." Our arrival had seemed to catch even the school board unaware. Swept up in preparation for a Japanese invasion, this little frontier town bustled with military and brimmed with VIPs. It was a miracle that we two *chechakoes* had found a little cabin to share that winter.

Gordon, the brash young man behind Polet's counter, had come north the year before to seek adventure. He wound up as a general handyman in the store, where everything from reindeer stew meat to walrus ivory to fine china could be bought. The place dated from the gold rush days of 1900.

Dorothy was a femme fatale. She soon established camaraderie with Gordon, and I tagged along, in awe of her tactics. One afternoon, as we entered the store, he opened negotiations. "Tonight's the night!"

"What's that?" inquired Dorothy, batting her eyelashes.

"Badminton. Every Monday night. It's mostly townspeople, but a few officers—and the general."

Wow! Gen. Jones, commanding officer in western Alaska! But neither Dorothy nor I played badminton very often, and besides that, we already had so many dates that we were almost too busy to even teach school.

But the repartee went on.

"Tonight's the night!" Dorothy would chirp, no matter what day she saw Gordon.

Then one day, I entered Polet's alone.

"Tonight's the night!" hailed Gordon. "I'll pick you up at 7:30, Shorty."

Shorty! How romantic. No one ever called me that. Could it be he liked me? So we went to badminton, and it had to be proof of Gordon's growing devotion: He struggled all winter to teach me to play. Optimistically, he called me "uncoordinated."

The season passed and spring 1943 arrived, along with the June boat, loaded with wonderful stuff like casserole dishes, bananas and nylons. The snow-blocked roads out of town were plowed open and summer came to the Arctic. And love! I ditched the GIs on my doorstep, and Gordon borrowed a decrepit old Ford. We rattled off into the countryside to fish and picnic. Although I can't stand fish, it was a fabulous courtship.

It's nice when a love story has a happy ending. But just when I wanted this guy, so did Uncle Sam. Instead of entering matrimony, Gordon entered military service. Although he was stationed at the Nome base, we didn't marry, for the Alaska Defense Command frowned on GI commitments. Couples who disregarded Army regulations found the bride soon on her way to the "lower 48." The Army brass didn't relent until late 1944, and we married in December.

There was a flip side to the happy ending, however. We rented a little cottage where I lived and to which Gordon commuted on the rare occasions when he was able to leave the base just outside town. But heavy winter storms conspired with the top sergeant in charge of passes to keep the roads blocked. Romantic candlelit dinners were infrequent. We spent our honeymoon on the telephone.

Some people remember 1945 as the year the war ended. As I remember, it was the year that our Arctic romance won out and Uncle Sam gave me back my man. ❖

Wedding Night Battle

By Faith W. Schremp

To say that our wedding night was extraordinary would be putting it mildly!

In September 1942, I left my job at a defense plant in Milwaukee. I had planned to work there for the duration of World War II. But my fiancé, whom I had known and loved since high school, was stationed at Camp Blanding, Fla., and he had telegraphed that I should come for a week's visit. He had made reservations for me in a guest house on the base.

I could not resist his invitation. I figured that if I lost my job over going, I'd find another. My job was important to me and to the war effort, but there was war work everywhere, and I could serve my country wherever I went. Besides, keeping up the morale of my serviceman was helping the war effort, too—not to mention what it did for my own morale.

After spending my allotted time in the guest house and enjoying the military atmosphere, I had to leave. My time was up. However, as you may have guessed, we changed our minds about waiting until the war was over to get married. The war might go on forever, and we decided, "Live today, for tomorrow we may die!" Many of my fiancé's GI buddies had already shipped over and had been killed. We planned to be married in the 313th Infantry chapel on the base, by the Army chaplain.

We found a trailer-house—not quite as elaborate as today's mobile homes, but very suitable for our needs. It was one of several in a temporary camp less than a mile outside the base.

Travel by train and bus was hectic in those days, expensive and crowded beyond description. Gas was rationed, and cars were in bad condition.

Then there came a rotten turn of events! C Company, in which my fiancé was a buck private, drew all the duties of "fire week" and was restricted to their area for the whole week. I would have to make all the wedding arrangements by myself. I had a visitor's pass and I could go into camp at designated times to compare notes with my fiancé. But our meetings were never private, and we felt like we were in a goldfish bowl every time!

Of course, it was better than nothing, since he could not come out to see me at all until noon of our wedding day. We were reminded that there was a war going on, and *that* came first.

All his buddies were grumbling, too. A wedding would have been cause for merriment and celebration for them, too, but they didn't see how they could pull it off with fire week restrictions. They felt they were being cheated by the war in this and in many other ways concerning their lives.

My fiancé got permission to leave his company and go to the chapel with one GI buddy to be his best man. The buddy's wife was my maid of honor, although I had never seen her before. No one from home would be able to come down. Travel by train and bus was hectic in those days, expensive and crowded beyond description. Gas was rationed, and cars were in bad condition, as no parts were available since all factories were making war equipment. It would be just us.

After the ceremony, by miracle of a special order in honor of the occasion, my husband was given a weekend pass. That pass gave us Saturday night and all day Sunday until 6 p.m., when he had to report back. We felt patriotic, so we accepted this as part of what we must put up with during wartime.

That night, we felt awed to actually be alone in our trailerhouse. Now that the big moment, our wedding night, had arrived, my husband and I looked at each other—wondering, I suppose, if it was real or a dream. Then suddenly both of us started laughing!

Along about 2 a.m., we were rudely awakened by the trailerhouse shuddering, banging and bumping. We had never experienced an earthquake before, but that's what we thought it had to be. The whole place creaked and groaned and shook so much that we almost fell out of bed.

Then we had another horrifying thought: Maybe we were under attack by our enemies! After all, we were at war!

"What in the world! …" my husband gasped after almost being thrown out of bed by the jolting. He grabbed his clothes and tried to get dressed as he was buffeted against the walls and furniture. What a racket!

I grabbed wildly for my robe, but everything danced and jiggled around me, and it kept slipping just out of my reach. I finally clutched it

Hurry-up weddings became popular during World War II as young people frantically grabbed whatever happiness they could find. Photo by Bernard Hoffman Circa 1942. Time Life Pictures/Getty Images

in a desperate swipe and managed to put it on while gruesome scenes of what could be happening out there flashed through my mind.

Suddenly, I thought of the GIs who were still restricted. That was it! They had come to make us pay for our freedom! They went over the fence!

Then I had another thought. It was Saturday night, and it was traditional for the soldiers to brawl in nearby Boomtown, a honky-tonk of questionable tenants and entertainment. Maybe it wasn't his company outside; maybe it was others, wandering around, looking for kicks! There were plenty of soldiers in Boomtown tonight, judging by the loud music and yelling and laughing and cursing that bombarded our ears. Boomtown could sell only "3.2 beer," but soldiers always had plenty of friends who supplied them with liquor. The MPs had their hands full and only managed to make token arrests.

My blood froze at the thought of drunken soldiers breaking into our flimsy trailer-house. No telling what they would do in their condition!

Then the trailer-house came to a standstill and it was deathly silent. My new husband and I stood motionless, eyes wide, listening. It was *too* quiet. Then we heard a series of snorts and grunts, groans and moans—and the banging and bumping and shaking resumed.

"We'll get killed—and on our wedding night!" I squeaked, grabbing my husband and clinging desperately to him. Then I had a brilliant idea. "At least we'll go together—not like you over there and me over here!" Somehow, though, even that thought, romantic as it had seemed, lost something in the verbalization. It did not comfort me—or him—in the least.

Gradually, my husband relaxed and a smile slowly spread over his face. "You know something?" he whispered as the trailer-house grew still again. "If that were GIs out there, they would have had the door busted in by now. I have a hunch—let's take a look."

Unable to even squeak anymore, as my voice had left me, I crowded close behind him as we stealthily crept to the door. My stomach was turning cartwheels. I could hear rustling outside, and once in a while a snort or grunt.

"We'll get killed—and on our wedding night!" I squeaked, grabbing my husband and clinging desperately to him. Then I had a brilliant idea.

They were regrouping to attack for real this time—I just knew it!

Suddenly, something hit the tiny window above our bed. I shuddered, ducked and covered my face. Then I heard my husband *laugh*! Quaking in fear, I warily uncovered my face and peeked out. There was the huge black and white face of a *cow*, butting her long horns on the window. Her eyes were wild and spooky, staring into the pale glimmer from the single weak light bulb in the ceiling of our honeymoon hideout. I gasped.

"There's your intruder!" My husband pointed at the cow and laughed hysterically. I was not quite convinced that this was all there was to it, but I was relieved—and then I felt *so* foolish!

"You knew it all the time!" I accused him, pummeling him with my fists as I began to laugh.

"No! I didn't really know until just now. But they do have freedom of the range out here. You'll see cows and pigs and chickens roaming all over, at will. No one bothers them, nor steals them—unless he wants to get hung! They don't have fences down here!"

Heaving a sigh of relief, we took a flashlight and gingerly stepped outside. Several cows were milling around. When they saw our flashlight, all of them turned their big, wild-looking eyes on us, like we were a target! I reached out to scratch the head of the one closest to us, wincing at the sight of her long, pointed horns. They were much longer than any I'd seen on cows back in Wisconsin! She had rubbed her itchy, hairy body against our trailer-home, causing most of the rumbling racket. In the light of the flashlight, we looked them over. On their hips they bore the brands of various owners.

It was 4 a.m. before the light went out again in our honeymoon trailer-house. ❖

Songs of Love

Love songs were the order of the day when wedding bells were ringing back in the Good Old Days. *Chapel of Love*, recorded in 1958 by The Dixie Cups, was a favorite among those who tied the knot.

Chapel of Love

Going to the chapel,
And we're gonna get married.
Going to the chapel
And we're gonna get married

Gee, I really love you,
And we're gonna get married.
Going to the chapel of love.

Spring is here.
The sky is blue.
Birds all sing
Like they do.
Today's the day
We'll say "I do,"
And we'll never be lonely anymore

Because we're
Going to the chapel,
And we're gonna get married.
Going to the chapel,
And we're gonna get married.

Gee, I really love you,
And we're gonna get married.
Going to the chapel of love.

Bells will ring.
The sun will shine.
I'll be his,
And he'll be mine.
We'll love until
The end of time,
And we'll never be lonely anymore.

Because we're
Going to the chapel,

And we're gonna get married.
Going to the chapel,
And we're gonna get married.
Gee, I really love you,
And we're gonna get married.
Going to the chapel of love.
Going to the chapel of love.
Going to the chapel of love.

Another favorite for newlyweds was *Yours*. The original title of this love song was *Quereme Mucho*. Composed in 1931 by Gonzalo Roig, the English words were written by Jack Sherr.

Yours

Yours 'til the stars lose their glory,
Yours 'til the birds fail to sing,
Yours to the end of life's story,
This pledge to you, dear, I bring.

Yours in the grey of December,
Here or on far distant shores,
I've never loved anyone the way I love you,
How could I, when I was born to be,
Just yours.

This night has music, the sweetest music,
It echoes somewhere within my heart,
I hold you near me, oh darling hear me,
I have a message I must impart,

Yours 'til the stars lose their glory,
Yours 'til the birds fail to sing,
Yours to the end of life's story,
This pledge to you, dear, I bring.

Yours in the grey of December,
Here or on far distant shores,
I've never loved anyone the way I love you,
How could I, when I was born to be,
Just yours,
Just yours,
When I was born to be just yours. ❖

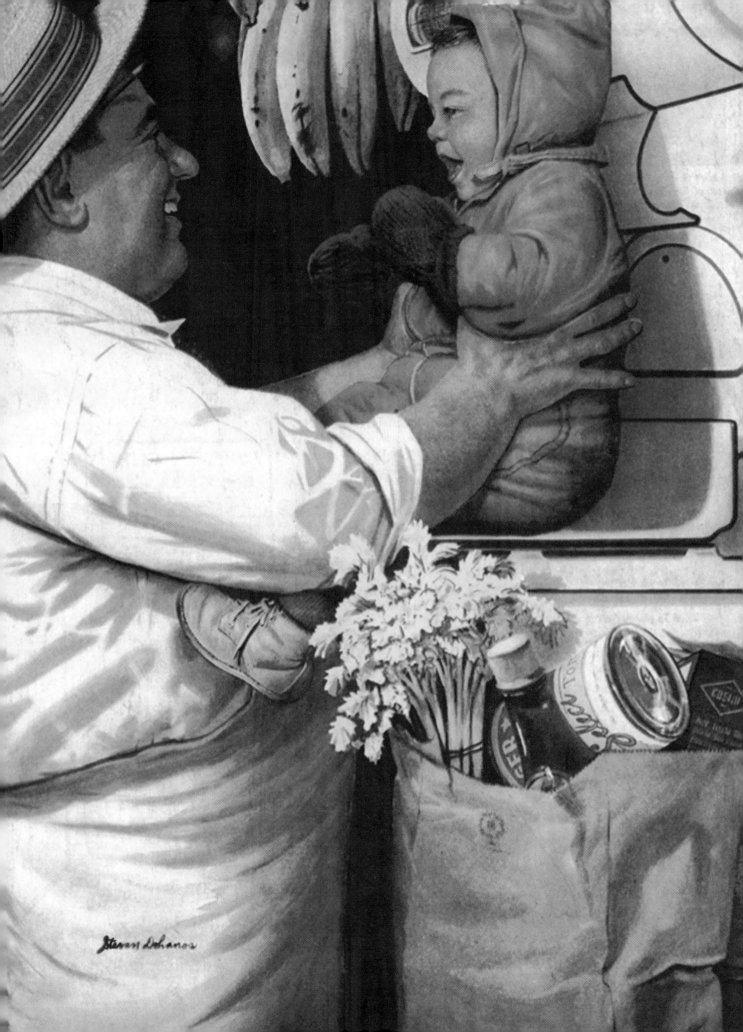

The Boom Years

Chapter Five

The exclamation point to the best years of our lives was the explosion of the boom years—an incredibly sweet time when we could again exuberantly sing, "Happy days are here again!"

The late 1940s and well into the 1950s were punctuated two distinct "booms."

The first boom was, obviously, the fruit of millions of new families growing a new generation of Americans. Some of the "Baby Boomers" resent being categorized that way, but it was exactly that—a baby boom—for so many of us.

Postwar days meant a time when the hardship of the rationing years was over. Hometown markets now were stocked with coffee and sugar, butter and beefsteak. It was becoming a lot easier to feed those Boom Years babies.

In those Good Old Days, a jovial grocer was not just a businessman—he was a good friend, too. I remember when our eldest son was born we didn't have a set of scales. Janice wanted to keep records of Junior's growth, so she unabashedly asked our local grocer to set him like a sack of potatoes on the grocery scales.

"Twelve pounds on the money, Miz Tate," he chortled. "Now, would you like a cut of stew meat to go with that?"

We were blessed with two daughters after that, but by then I could afford conveniences like bathroom scales. To the best of my knowledge Janice never had to resort to the hometown market meat scales again.

The second boom was that of the job market. One of the first of a large extended family to have the opportunity to go to college, I enjoyed a career in newspapers and higher education. After the war, most of us could find jobs. The Depression was over and we were on the threshold of great times. The booming economy financed our booming families.

The boom years were the climax of all that had gone before. Johnny had come marching home. Once there he was able to finish school, find a good job and marry the girl of his dreams. The picture was completed with the joyful addition of children.

No, life was not perfect. World conflict was over, but the Cold War was just beginning. Soon we would have young men fighting in the Korean War. The pall of the atomic threat hung over us, and our children grew up learning about bomb shelters and nuclear fallout.

But those years were filled with innocence and Howdy Doody and coonskin caps and *Mr. Sandman*. Despite the problems still out there, those Boom Years made us believe we must be living in the best years of our lives.

—*Ken Tate*

No Babies Allowed!

By Audrey Carli

The day we turned the calendar to the month of August 1952 started with a soft breeze blowing through our kitchen window in the old Milwaukee neighborhood. Dave, my husband, and I were stunned when our silky smooth schedule was smashed later that afternoon.

My college-student husband and I had been excited by plans to prepare for our first baby's birth when autumn leaves would be falling. Our anticipation was so keen that we felt optimistic about our ability to cope with our rising living costs, included Dave's college fees. We had each other, and soon we would welcome our firstborn.

The day grew hot and humid while I was at work and Dave was at his summer job at the frozen-food plant, but I stayed cheerful. Although housing where babies were welcome was scarce, we were secure in having a place that allowed a child.

Some couples we knew had been turned away from furnished apartments and had been told, "No babies allowed here." We felt sorry for them. Our friends, Marlene and Joe, lived apart after their baby, Lee, was born. Marlene returned to her northern Wisconsin hometown with the baby to live temporarily with her parents. Joe rented a room and visited his family on occasional weekends.

We planned to stay in our apartment for two more years, until Dave finished college and became a teacher. But that plan changed when it hit a snag, shattering our contentment in our third-floor walk-up in the converted mansion on North 25th Street.

On that hot August day, I was walking up the stairs after work to relax with the paper before starting supper. Suddenly I stopped on the third-floor landing and listened! Something was buzzing loudly inside our apartment!

I jerked the door open to find two men in work denims sawing away one of the walls! Plaster chunks were strewn everywhere! "What's going on?" I gasped.

"The landlord will tell you. We're putting a fire escape between your living room-bedroom here and the kitchen. You'll have to go into the hallway to get between the rooms when we finish this job."

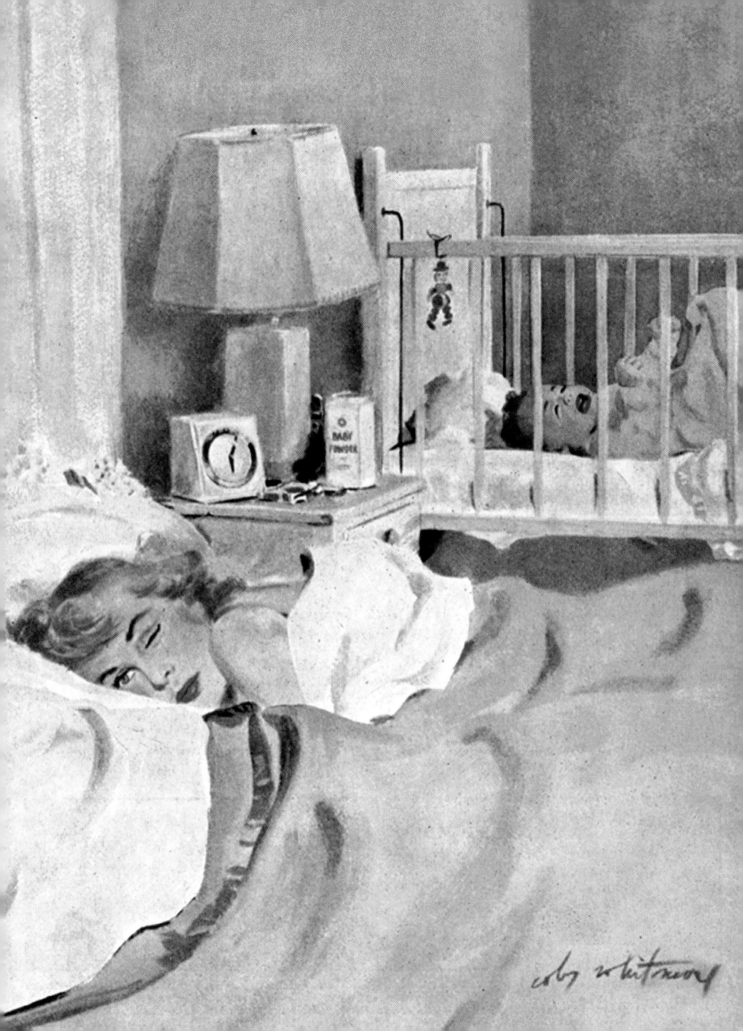

How would we tend a newborn if we had to leave one part of the apartment to get to the other?

Later, Dave and I realized that we had no choice but to stay with the mess. "We don't want to be split up when our baby arrives the way Joe and Marlene are," Dave said with a sigh.

So we cleaned up the plaster chunks and dust for several evenings after work. Our sweaty clothes were plastered to us as we tidied the place in the sweltering heat. But when we felt the grit of plaster dust between our teeth as we ate—despite tight-fitting food covers—we started circling "apartment for rent" ads right away!

Apartment hunting was a challenge. We walked the streets in our spare time, hoping to see "For Rent" signs in windows. That was a common way back then to advertise vacancies.

My hopes rose when a kindly older woman led me to the second floor of her brick building. She showed me a tidy, two-room place with reasonable rent. But when she realized we were expecting a baby, she frowned. "I hope you understand. We can't rent to you. Other tenants need to sleep. Some even sleep days if they work nights." I nodded, sighed and kept searching.

My hopes leaped again when I saw the sign in the front window of a drab, two-story house on busy Highland Avenue. The sign read: "Furnished Apartment for Rent—Child Welcome."

One look at that apartment told me that few would choose to live there unless they were desperate—but we were desperate! The furnished kitchen and living room-bedroom combination displayed limp, gray curtains that had once been white, dusty walls and gritty floors. But hope brightened my viewpoint. In my mind's eye, I saw the apartment cleaned up and cozy. "I think we'll want it, but my husband has to see it first," I told Mrs. Miller, the smiling landlady.

Later, Dave looked at the apartment I had described to him with more zeal than the drab place deserved. He scanned it in silence. Then Dave whispered to me after Mrs. Miller left us

The older woman showed me a tidy, two-room place with reasonable rent. But when she realized we were expecting a baby, she frowned. "I hope you understand. We can't rent to you. Other tenants need to sleep."

alone to answer her phone. "We can't live here," he protested. "It's on the corner of two busy streets. The traffic will keep us awake. I wonder why it was shown before it was cleaned?"

"A baby being welcomed was enough, I guess," I whispered. "The two of us could clean it, right?"

"It looks hopeless, Honey. I want a better place for you and our baby. Maybe I should get a job and finish college some other time."

"I see the dirt," I whispered, "but we have energy, soap and God-given strength. I want to help clean it!"

Dave shrugged and smiled. "I'm willing to clean this place, too. But it'll take both of us with our schedules."

"We're healthy and strong. We'll make this place cozy!" I hoped and prayed my words would come to pass.

Mrs. Miller's dark eyes widened, then shimmered when we agreed to rent the shabby abode. "You can move in anytime," she lilted.

We moved in, and with a borrowed vacuum cleaner, soap, water and much energy, we got rid of the dirt. We cheered up the place with old but neat curtains from our parents' attics. And we added a homey touch with a lush, green philodendron from Woolworth's variety store.

Our victory was complete when we looked at our clean-smelling, bright-walled, spotless-floored haven. When our baby girl, Debbie, was born, she joined us in our cozy home, and we were indeed a happy family.

Each time friends visited, they made comments like "How did you find such a cute place?" We smiled and agreed that we were fortunate to have found our little home.

Time passed and we moved to the Michigan town where Dave taught social studies to the seventh and eighth grades. Later we bought a home where we welcomed three more children: Glenn, Lynn and Lori.

Our contentment bloomed during those early times in the baby boom years. And the memories still add spice to our lives! ❖

Chasing Boom Times

By Dale Geise

Since I had just graduated from Underwood High School in southwestern Iowa in 1946, I was not a World War II veteran coming home to boom times. To search for that season, I would have to wait for another war.

My whole life had been spent on a farm until 1945, when my father, Arthur, suddenly decided to move to town and become a custom baler, corn sheller and corn picker. He chose that life and loved it. Among my favorite memories of him is the image of him standing erect at the steering wheel of his John Deere "A" tractor mounted with his pride, a two-row corn picker. He comes crashing through the stalks, dry leaves flying, and a shower of yellow ears spouting into the trailing wagon. His Thermos of scalding-hot coffee—in cold weather and in 100-degree summer baling weather alike—is tucked into a homemade toolbox under the seat. He also liked to pose for photos beside his truck-mounted corn sheller with a grandchild in the crook of his arm. The white board sign fixed on the cab top read "Uncle Artie Geise—Corn Shelling."

His pleasure in that work was balanced against my emptiness. My long apprenticeship with every kind of farm fieldwork and chores was ending, and I was ready to emerge as a very junior partner in the burgeoning farm community soon to come. Then my brother, Dudley, was off to the Air Force, and my dad left the farm.

To get near the fields again, I worked for dear friends, Albert and Gertrude Peterson. I almost became a third son in their family of two small boys and a girl. We farmed "Mount Baldy" and "Mount Beastly," as Albert christened their steep sides. We laughed to think of livestock grazing there with legs longer on one side to accommodate the challenging slopes. I stood on the flanks of those "mountains" and moved upgrade and down, holding a straight 5-foot stick while Albert balanced a carpenter's level on another stick and sighted in a contour line for the corn rows—the first contoured crops in our neighborhood.

Albert's love of the land affected me deeply. His patience taught me to be calm in a storm. For instance, a teenager, full of hurry and energy, might drive the tractor away from an elevated gas tank, leaving the long supply hose with its spout still stuck in the tractor tank. A sharp "pop" might separate the hose from the tank, leaving a forceful stream of gas pouring out on the ground.

In the midst of my dismay, Albert was serenely quiet and composed. He was tested again when I upended a 5-gallon can of gas, sticking the can nozzle into the tractor tank opening, as I had done a hundred times. It works well except when the tractor has just stopped running, is still hot, and catches fire. But Albert's patience never wavered. I will never stop thanking his memory for helping me through those trying times and for all the goodness that was showered on me by that loving family in my time of need.

> *After discharge in late 1952, I could have, and perhaps would have, gone right back to being a farmhand, but the GI Bill plucked me up and set me on the road to college.*

Farming the "mountains" in summer left the winter for odd jobs, writing stories, and one of the sweet loves of my life—basketball! Every little hamlet in that part of the state had a team. After high school, I played for McClelland. The tops of our uniforms were blue undershirts with red felt letters *glued* to the front! Neola, Persia, Portsmouth, Hancock, Carson, Macedonia and Treynor also took small-town pride in their local boys playing basketball.

In January 1949, 25 teams converged on Minden for the Southwest Iowa Independent Basketball Tournament, and $475 in cash prizes! Small towns were renewing their energy as young veterans came home to help aging parents on the farms. Sixty-five businesses placed 2-inch or larger box ads in the tournament program. There was some "booming" going on!

Among the advertisers there were creameries and "Quick Lunches," implement dealers and individual livestock truckers, hatcheries, feed dealers, taverns and doctors and dentists. Four funeral homes from Council Bluffs filled the final ad page—perhaps a somber note, but reassuring to young men not fully conditioned by a winter of milking and choring. If a mishap should occur in the middle of a modest fast break, they would be well cared for to the end.

I spent many winter afternoons calling politely but urgently to ask for the use of the Underwood gym. Our Quonset hut practice gym and city hall in McClelland was too claustrophobic for game action.

There were calls to arrange for referees and a check-off up and down our variegated roster to find the minimum five willing to do battle for McClelland. I was automatically available and would cheerfully have paid to play the game that had a secure grasp on my heart.

When Russian tanks rolled down the Korean peninsula, my future changed. At Fort Leonard Wood in Missouri, I got ready to serve in the First Cavalry Division and the Third Division in Korea. I sat on many a hill in that devastated country dreaming of a white bread, mustard and baloney

I climbed mountains and canoed lakes with a dignified and unforgettable older co-leader and dozens of fine, clear-eyed New York city boys whose names and faces remain with me.

sandwich and clean white bed sheets—and basketball. I ponder still that in the midst of wreckage and darkness, the mind will turn to needs so simple.

After discharge in late 1952, I could have, and perhaps would have, gone right back to being a farmhand, but the GI Bill plucked me up and set me on the road to college. At the University of Iowa, there were few days between classes that I didn't work at cleaning barns, handling eggs or painting rooms for elderly ladies who rented rooms to students. I hand-waxed huge cars at a gas station at night and filled in as assistant recreation director for the city of Iowa City. Summers found me shoveling mud at a power plant, or on a railroad track crew, or driving a night taxi in Omaha, Neb. Still, the GI Bill was the foundation of my finances.

One special attempt to lock in on the financial boom times came with my "Thousand Pheasants Project." Those thousand chicks came from the Engebretson Game Farms in Chariton, Iowa, and were raised in a willow-pole and chicken-wire pen on my parents' small acreage. I made a modest profit, but still, the boom eluded me.

In my last college summer, I answered an ad for Raquette Lake Boys Camp in the Adirondack Mountains of New York state. It was a long drive out there and back for a $300 salary and a modest travel expense. The postwar economy still was not filling my pockets. But far greater rewards were stamped on my life and memory in an account that can never be spent. I climbed mountains and canoed lakes with a dignified and unforgettable older co-leader and dozens of fine, clear-eyed New York city boys whose names and faces remain with me.

The lessons of work I learned on the farm led to graduation and 33 years of teaching good kids, always hoping to help them have a better chance to succeed along the road of life. Those days left me rich with rewards that have no pay window.

I have a great love for those late 1940s and all the 1950s. Always, they seemed to me to be times of quiet hope and optimism. I want to remember them that way. ❖

Mother's Best Years

By Edna Krause

World War II was over and it seemed the sun shone brighter and birds sang sweeter. No more red tokens for soap and gasoline. The shelves were full of Rinso White and Oxydol and I didn't need to make my own soap from lye and lard.

Sher, my husband, found a teaching job in Sebewaing, a small town on Lake Huron in Michigan. Some said Sebewaing had been built on land once covered by Lake Huron. No wonder the soil was black and fertile, ideally suited for growing sugar beets.

However, I wasn't suited to my new postwar life as wife and mother. I had never learned how to cook, sew, or even how to hold a newborn baby. Now, miles from family and with not one friend in Sebewaing, I wondered how I was going to take care of a baby and manage a home.

But in 1947, when the country returned to a peacetime economy, I had many ways to ease my concerns.

The war plants were again producing cars, and we ordered our first brand-new car. Sher refused to buy another used car after our last one burned more oil than gasoline and black, smelly smoke trailed behind us everywhere we drove. Sher carried two or three gallons of used oil in the trunk of that car and added it to the motor every so often. The garage mechanics were only too happy to give him their used oil.

At last, after waiting for two months, our new beige Chevrolet stood in our dirt driveway.

No garage came with our tiny house, and I mean tiny. The old one-story house was only 20 by 20 feet.

But how happy and proud we were of our first house and first new car!

In our joy, we didn't mind the steady lines of trucks carrying sugar beets idling in front of our house or rumbling by from early morning until late at night. Most of October and November they carried sugar beets to the sugar processing factory. Our neighbors, having lived in this sugar beet town for years, were more accustomed to the blocked driveways and truck-rutted lawns.

But who cared about ruts in the yard when the "boys" were home and the country was getting back to a peacetime economy? We worked all day and danced to *Blue Skirt Waltz* and *Cruising Down the River* at night.

Like most women around 1948, I was a stay-at-home mom. Our youngest child was born while we lived in Sebe-

Edna with her husband Sher, and young son Ron, at the time of this story.

waing. With Jimmy's birth, we had added two children to the nation's baby boomer population. By now I had become an old pro at motherhood and I was quite pleased with myself.

On a sunny, bird-song day, the streets were filled with smiling, chatty mothers pushing buggies. I remember the used buggy Sher bought for our first son, Ron. He painted the wicker buggy light brown and I made blue padding to fit around the inside. I used that same buggy for Jim.

Sometimes I held Jim on my lap when we took our sons for rides along the Lake Huron shore. These shores, where a person could wade out an eighth of a mile, were a fisherman's paradise all summer. And every fall, duck hunters came from miles around to try their luck.

Sher hated to give up the good fishing and hunting, but eventually we left Sebewaing for Muskegon. Sher had spent part of his childhood in Muskegon, so he wanted to return to the city he liked. It had grown considerably during World War II, when workers from the South were brought to Muskegon to fill jobs in the foundries and steel mills.

My first impression of Muskegon was not very favorable, however. It seemed the streets were filled with old, rusty cars chugging along. Soon, however, all that would change. The economy had begun to boom along with the baby population. Factories hummed day and night to fill orders for cars, refrigerators, stoves and small appliances.

Sher found a job teaching woodshop in Muskegon and worked at the Anaconda factory on weekends. Soon we had enough money to buy a brand-new house that was much larger than our first home. We bought many appliances that we had never had before.

I was awed by all the "property" I now owned. We even had a paved driveway! How the children enjoyed playing on it with the toys their dad made for them! Sher and I enjoyed sitting on the porch and watching our pre-schoolers as they rode the wooden train and tractor he had made.

I never tired of being a stay-at-home mom. Little

by little, I gained confidence in mothering and my apprehension turned to joy and satisfaction. At the close of day, it felt cozy to sit on the floor as Sher and I watched our children play with Tinker Toys.

It was fun taking the boys to Wolf Lake or Lake Michigan for a refreshing dip and then making sand castles in the warm sun. Every morning I woke up the brothers by saying, "Get up 3-year-old, get up 5-year-old," or whatever their age was at the time. I went through this ritual because I wanted to hold back time and keep them in their tender baby years. I suspected that they would bring me the greatest joy while they were still "Mama's boys." Soon friends would become important and they would begin to break away from their parents.

In spite of the great sacrifices we made during the war (some more than others), I was able to focus on what I had now that the war was over. I'm glad I savored the moments during our sons' early childhood and elementary school years. Now, as I look back, the early years of motherhood were my best. ❖

1947 Youngstown Kitchens by Mullins ad, House of White Birches nostalgia archives

The Courtship of Ruby & Ewing

By Opal Chadwick Blaylock

I was a 10-year-old girl living in Independence County in rural Arkansas, when World War II exploded into my tranquil, carefree world. Before I could begin to comprehend the meaning of the word "war," my playmates' brothers, as well as my own, were being called away.

Mail started to arrive in our little post office from training camps all over the United States. Little banners appeared in windows all across town, bearing a blue star for every military man who had left that home. Some banners had four or more stars! Church pews were left empty. Fields were not plowed and weeds grew in places where corn and cotton once had thrived.

I lived with a secret fear that the Japanese would enter our country and hide in our barn. I even checked out the woodshed to make sure no enemy lurked there. My understanding of the atrocities of war was limited, but I knew war was real and deadly.

Letters replaced Sunday-afternoon dates for my older sisters and their friends. One sad December day in 1944, a visitor came with news that my sister Joyce's fiancé had been killed. Friends rallied around her in loving support and reached out to Rudean's family as well.

Every victory in battle became a milestone. Everyone hoped and prayed for the wonderful day when the killing would stop. We cheered the newsreels shown at the movies.

Then the day came when letters began to arrive bearing the addresses of bases in the United States instead of "in care of" post office boxes. This was a sign to the home folks that their loved ones were returning. Soon after, one by one, the boys started coming home. Some came limping or moving like old men, a far cry from the spry young men they had been when they left. Their beards were heavier, their voices deeper, and their conversations more sober. Neighbor boys came to visit my family when they returned home. As they shook my daddy's hand, tears filled their eyes and a handshake became an embrace.

One day, Ewing Miller came to see us. My folks had known Ewing for many years. He was not a big man, but was what my daddy called "wiry" and steady. I could tell he had a special place with my daddy. He was a little older than some of the other returning heroes. I noticed that he came more often than the others, too.

Soon after he returned to Hot Springs, Ark., where he was undergoing treatment for "jungle rot" on his feet, letters started coming from him addressed to my older sister Ruby. I usually brought the mail up from the mailbox, but now Ruby started making the trip ahead of me. She seemed anxious to get the mail.

I couldn't have been happier if this was happening to me. This Ewing was the brother of my great friend, Maxine! After all the awful days of war and shortages (no bubble gum!), very little fun and much too much work, things were looking rosy!

Maxine and I really took an interest in the courtship of Ruby and Ewing. After all, we were young, starry-eyed teenagers, and we were ready to milk this for all it was worth.

Ewing came home on a weekend pass every few weeks. He and Ruby saw a lot of each other, but they never went out. He was still limping, and he didn't have transportation.

Then one weekend, not long before he was discharged, Ewing roared up our driveway in a little Ford car with a rumble seat. I have no idea what year or model it was, but it ran, and that was all that mattered!

Maxine hadn't known he was getting a car. In fact, she was not getting much information at all. It seemed his older sister had a friend she wanted him to date. He was being real hush-hush about his relationship with Ruby.

Maxine and I did get the word that they were planning to go to the Saturday-night late show in Batesville. This show was known as the "owl" show. The way I found out about it was quite simple.

My sister had very bad hair. It was fine, thin and straight as a board. I was good with bobby pins, so she enlisted me to fix her hair for their date. Always mindful of a bargain, I negotiated a ride into town in the rumble seat for Maxine and me on Saturday night.

I soon discovered that I had not made a glowing deal. Getting that stubborn hair to wave, curl or even bend was almost impossible, and we had no hair spray or setting gel to help. But I put forth my best effort and dared her to move her head or put it on his shoulder until after the show.

Of course, they put their stipulations on Maxine and me, too. We could ride into town, but we had to disappear until we reconnected at the agreed-upon location five or 10 minutes after the show was over. And once we were home, we had to go inside without peeping out the window or even looking back on our way into the house.

This setup worked well for some time, even if I did have to pay a high price for it. I often had to assist Ruby with her dress as well as her hair. I think she squealed, too, because Maxine got pressed into service: She had to shine Ewing's shoes for the date. They did take us to a few church functions "for free," but I was afraid that even *that* might backfire and we'd get hit with more blackmail!

Then, late that fall, we began getting vibes that the situation was about to change, and it didn't look like a win-win situation for us. Ruby got real quiet. She seemed distracted. One time she made a peach pie and forgot to serve it. She ironed a dress, then put it back in the dirty clothes. And Maxine said that Ewing read the same two pages of a book for two or three days.

We didn't want them to break up. We had no idea of what had happened. We hadn't thought far enough ahead to think of marriage, but *they* had! They told Mama and Daddy and his folks the next Sunday: They were planning to get married in January.

Oh, boy, there goes the rumble seat! Now Maxine and I would have to make other arrangements. But being of dating age ourselves by now, we figured that we could find a way into our own courting situations.

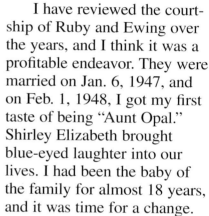

I have reviewed the courtship of Ruby and Ewing over the years, and I think it was a profitable endeavor. They were married on Jan. 6, 1947, and on Feb. 1, 1948, I got my first taste of being "Aunt Opal." Shirley Elizabeth brought blue-eyed laughter into our lives. I had been the baby of the family for almost 18 years, and it was time for a change.

Then, on May 16, 1950, the day before I graduated from high school, Ewing Junior brought a serious, gentle little grin to make our day.

Ruby and Ewing raised two great kids who grew up to be two great people. Both became schoolteachers and added to the lives of many. They bring joy to my heart to this very day. My telephone will ring and one of them will ask, "Aunt Opal, how are you doing?" You can bet I am just fine.

It took a few years for my returning soldier to find me, but he became my husband and a beloved uncle to Shirley and Junior. One of the oft-repeated family stories is about our visit to Ruby and Ewing's home shortly after we married. We moved from the small town to the city to be near my husband's work. The children were playing near a window when Junior asked his sister and cousin, "Who is that man with Aunt Opal?"

His 3-year-old cousin, Cathy, proudly proclaimed, "Oh, Junior, she lives with him now!"

As I review the years since World War II, I realize that it takes more than war, illness or death to break the ties that bind a family that has stood together for God and country, a family that has stood together in times of sorrow and in times of jubilation. ❖

A Brand-New World

By Alice C. Orshall

*I*t was a brand-new world to which our GIs came home after World War II—a whole different culture, as far as social status was concerned. Homes and neighborhoods we never dreamed of living in became available to all of us, thanks to the GI Bill.

Now the banker's daughter, attorneys, mayors and the timekeeper from the local smelter all shared equal status, and our common bond was our children. From newborns to those of baseball-playing age, they all seemed to love to gather in our yards. And it seemed like most everyone got along. No one was rich, but neither were they poor.

Then along came television. On warm summer evenings after dinner, we would stream from all our homes and gather in a joyous crowd with one goal in mind: North End Radio, with its large, magical TV in the front window. On the sidewalk we would gather in a huge semicircle to view the magic of TV. Arthur Godfrey in black and white was really something. All the performers' lips looked black, but the jokes and music came through loud and clear. We even joined in as singers, including Jeannette Davis, performed the latest songs from the top of the Hit Parade.

We stood there until the sky began to darken and the street lights came on. Still reluctant to go home, we trooped across the street and filled the dining room at Knapp's Restaurant, where they made the best homemade pie in town. Finally, with full tummies and sleepy kids, we trooped back home, only to repeat the whole process a few days later.

> *Ah, the TV bug bit us, and bit us hard—and almost before we knew it, we had succumbed and bought the first TV set in our neighborhood. Now our neighbors' destination switched from the radio store to our home.*

Ah, but the TV bug bit us, and bit us hard—and almost before we knew it, we had succumbed and bought the first TV set in our neighborhood. Now our neighbors' destination switched from the radio store to our home.

At first, the novelty of it was wonderful. My husband was eager to show it off and explain it to everyone. And as for me—well, I prepared snack after snack, day after day and week after week. No one else thought to offer to help.

But in every neighborhood, there is one person—or one family—who always likes to play "We Can Top This." And they did. Their TV was much bigger and better than ours, and the exodus quickly swung across the street and up the block to their house.

I smiled to myself, although I was a little ashamed that I hadn't warned them about the river of treats people would expect them to provide.

So, quietly and contentedly, my family lived alone, happily ever after. ❖

Children sit captivated by the television screen. Circa 1957. Hulton Archives/Getty Images

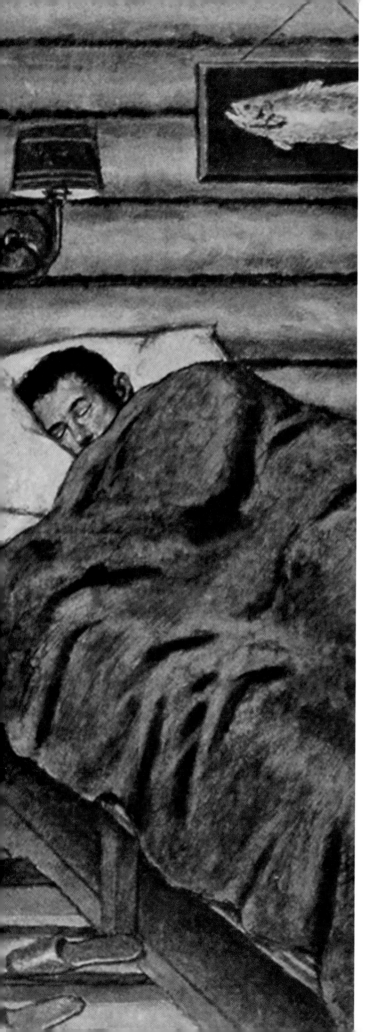

Best Days Of My Life

By Edna Krause

very spring I yearned for a summer home somewhere in a sun-kissed field near a deep, dark forest and a tinkling stream. My husband, Sher, an avid fisherman, also wanted to escape the city. It was possible to nurture our dream because he was a teacher, and summer was a time of no work—and no pay.

But our plans always evaporated. We chickened out because we didn't know if we really could handle leaving our modern home and living a rustic life for nine weeks. And it would be much more difficult to find a summer job if we tired of camping after only two weeks.

I also wondered if our sons, Ron and Jim, would be happy without daily calls for a game of baseball or marbles from their city friends. So we decided not to disclose our plans to our sons until we were certain of what we wanted to do.

Finally, during the spring of 1954, Sher's enthusiasm boiled over. He spoke of nothing but a carefree summer in Michigan's cool forests and rushing rivers. "I'll fish every day," he proclaimed, grinning from ear to ear.

Hearing something about fishing, Ron and Jim came running out of their bedroom. Eyes sparkling and smiling, they listened. Then 11-year-old Ron interrupted, "Let's go! I want to fish and look for tackle in the shallow rivers."

"And I'm taking my BB gun and hunting down rabbit and deer in case the fish aren't biting," gushed 9-year-old Jim.

I listened to all the enthusiasm and suddenly it occurred to me that I didn't want to live in a tent for nine weeks. "Nine weeks is a long time to live with bugs in a tent," I said.

"I've been thinking about that, too," Sher said, smiling. "Let's buy an old house trailer!"

The day after school was out in June, we pulled our 20-foot house trailer north to "where the big ones were biting." We left behind friends and city life with all its conveniences—phone, radio, lights, running water, heat and electricity. We took along a wind-up clock and a calendar. And, oh yes, the trailer came with a small propane gas tank for cooking.

We stayed in many county and state parks in Lower Michigan. In the early 1950s, rustic parks were equipped only with a pump and bathroom. There were no fire pits or firewood waiting for the campers. And no fees to pay, either. All we had to do was sign a paper at the park entrance.

At our first stop, Bray Creek Campground, Sher found a level spot with no trees and backed our house trailer onto it. We blocked the wheels and secured our belongings. Then we scattered in all directions like hatchery fingerlings dumped into a river.

I should write here that in the early 1950s, people didn't flock to rustic parks for camping. All week long we were alone in the park. Only on weekends did we see one or two anglers trying their luck.

But that's the way we liked it. Sher lived his dream of fishing every day. And I was born to live in harmony with nature's quiet beauty, using skills I had learned from years of farm living.

At times I wondered if our sons' contentment would last the entire nine weeks. True, they were the best of friends, always together, even in the city. Every day, arm in arm, they left the trailer to explore their surroundings. They found a million things to do besides fishing with their dad. They built a lean-to out of dead wood. They climbed trees and built a stone dam across Bray Creek. Then they dismantled the dam and looked for gold under the rocks. Every day brought new adventures.

While we were camped at Old Grade Park, they built a raft using logs they found alongside the river and rope their dad carried in our station wagon. How proud they looked as they floated down the Little Manistee River!

I brought along a kerosene lamp, but I needn't have bothered; we were all in bed before the last ray of light left the western sky. The fresh air and activity in the warm sun made all of us sleep like contented babies.

Most mornings, Sher slipped out to the river before the first ray of sunshine peered into our house trailer. Much later, the boys bounced out of bed and rushed out to the pump to get fresh water to drink. As I prepared breakfast, I heard the squeaky pump handle and water splashing into the bucket. I bent a wire clothes hanger and set it over a burner with the gas turned low to make a makeshift toaster for my homemade bread. "Smells toasty good," Ron said as he heaved the pail of water up onto the counter. Eggs crackled in the frying pan as I set out the juicy, wild raspberries we had picked the day before.

After breakfast, I dipped water out of the pail into the kettle. Soon whistling, swirling steam told me I had hot water for doing dishes.

I hung the wet dish towel on the line Ron had strung from tree to tree. The boys hung wet towels there, too, after swimming or wading. And that's where Sher's wet socks hung if a hole developed in his hip boots during the day.

Because we were miles from a store and determined to "live off the land," most of our meals were pioneer-style. Our shelves held only nonperishable foods, supplemented by what we found in the wild.

Ron, Jim and I never tired of hunting for wild apples, raspberries, blueberries and gooseberries. We loved tramping through the clover-scented fields and suddenly discovering a patch of plump, sweet berries. Near the Pine River, at Silver Creek Park, we came upon a patch of raspberries so abundant that we picked four quarts.

And most every noon, hip-booted Sher, tackle dangling from his vest and hat, came home carrying a string of trout. Trout was our favorite fish. And it was a good thing, too, because we had small helpings of trout almost every day—and sometimes twice a day, since we had no refrigeration. Little Jimmy didn't need to hunt rabbits or deer with his BB gun to put meat on the table.

The nine weeks were coming to a close. Many times I found myself thinking, *These are some of the best days of my life.* Not one of us said we were anxious to leave our rustic life and return to the city. In fact, we spent four more summers in Michigan's beautiful parks. ❖

Our Waterworks

By Mildred Mitchell

I'm through! I've been promoted!" That was my husband's brother, Donald Mitchell, the future head of the State Sanitary Board of South Dakota, dancing around our kitchen, waving his government check over his head. He had reason to be happy. We all did. We were ready to install our indoor plumbing.

We bought our first home in Osceola County in the middle of Michigan in 1950. Most available houses had been built before indoor plumbing, telephones and electricity came to our part of the state. Our house came with a small shed where the former owners had raised chickens, a pump in the back yard, an outhouse farther out and a cedar hedge along the driveway. The most modern item in our new home was the oil burner in the middle of the dining room that, along with the wood-burning cookstove in the kitchen, was our only source of heat during snowy Michigan winters. We did have electricity.

We fell in love with the hedge and treated the rest of the place like a bride treats a new husband: We couldn't wait to change it.

Off to the local lumberyard we went with our list of copper pipe, plumbing fixtures and various incidentals such as nuts, bolts, heavy lengths of galvanized pipe and special wrenches and tools we needed to install inside plumbing.

Factories in our end of the world were still struggling to catch up with civilian needs after having been converted to war production at the beginning of World War II. Jobs were plentiful. Most of my women friends had found baby sitters and had gone to work, and they used their paychecks to modernize their homes. The demand for parts and fixtures was far ahead of the supply. "Sure," we were told. "Leave your order and as soon as we catch up, we'll send the stuff right out to you. You want the bill now or when we deliver the goods?"

"Now," we said together.

"Well, the price may change a bit," said the clerk, "but I can give you a pretty fair estimate if you wait while I figure it up."

We waited. The estimate was three times what we had expected. Still, we put the order on hold and hoped we could find the money to pay for it by the time it arrived. "Get by as best you can and wait," we were advised. As if we had a choice!

Veterans of World War II were awarded government-guaranteed loans for homes and schooling. We bought the house and Donald took both the schooling and a house in Lansing, Mich. Their house had a telephone and indoor plumbing.

Our house cost $3,500. The payback was $25 per month. We could get along fine as long as circumstances did not change. Of course, they did. One June morning, after a long night, we found ourselves the parents of a little boy. We had no memory of ordering a little boy, but we were happy to keep him. But suddenly we needed furniture for another bedroom and a bigger car; Pa needed a better job and Ma needed another pair of hands and eyes. We put the plumbing on hold.

We found a used washing machine and a fist-sized gadget that plugged into the electric

> *Our house cost $3,500.*
> *The payback was $25 per month.*
> *We could get along fine as long*
> *as circumstances did not change.*
> *Of course, they did.*

light socket to heat the water we pumped and lugged in by the bucketful at night. We plugged in the cord and dropped the little heater into the tub. By the next morning the water would be hot. With a hand-cranked wringer and more tubs of icy water for rinsing, we dealt with the white flannel squares that seemed to flap on the clothesline as often as they decorated the business end of our little boy. (Throw-away diapers had not yet been heard of.) "It'll get better," we told ourselves. We saved every nickel we could and checked every day to see if the plumbing fixtures had arrived. They hadn't.

Gasoline rationing during the war kept the mileage down on automobiles, but with highway maintenance on country roads at a dead stand-still, cars still got pretty beat up. We bought a 1945 Plymouth sedan for $300. Husband Ernie found a job working for the county highway department at $1.05 per hour. Between the

house payment of $25 a month and the car payment of $10 a month, the plumbing had to be put on hold. Again!

Somehow, though, when most of the parts we had ordered finally arrived, we had saved enough money to pay for them.

Installing a septic tank involves digging a mighty big hole. The only spot to install it was in a corner between the hedge and the kitchen. It was too small a space for any big equipment, so the hole had to be dug by hand, with a shovel.

Donald graduated from Michigan State College about that time and headed to Michigan's Upper Peninsula to do his apprenticeship for his veterinarian's license. His small stipend from the government, due a few days after graduation, was late. "For room and board, I'll dig the hole for the septic tank," he offered. So he and wife, Hazel, and two children moved in.

"Just until the check comes," we agreed.

"I'll dig after work at night," said Ernie. "We'll get Roy to help." Roy was their younger brother.

So dig they did. It was July and we had had no rain for weeks. The clay soil was hard as iron. Every shovelful had to be pounded loose with a pick before it could be shoveled out. Don rose early and pounded all day in the broiling sun. By lunchtime he was scalded with sweat, and most of his clothing was piled around the hole, which was barely inches deeper than it had been the day before.

Roy had his own farming to attend to, but he came when he could. We prayed for rain to soften the ground. It never came. When the hole got deep enough to hurt someone who might fall in, they covered it up at night with boards.

"Who are you setting a trap for?" laughed John and Nellie Harris, our nearest neighbors. John gave everyone a nickname, so the brothers were soon being referred to as "the Three Wise Men." Donald was "Wise," for he had graduated from college. Ernie was "Wiser," for he left for his job each morning and avoided the digging for a few hours. Brother Roy was "Otherwise," for he did whatever he was ordered to do, and John said he didn't need to know anything. They took it all with good humor, for they were too tired to argue.

The men's aunt, Katie Conkell, came one evening to inspect the job. She walked through a hole in the hedge, stepped on a weak board, and down she went! The hole was still only about a foot deep, and she was not seriously injured, but her yelling alerted the neighbors and created lots of excitement as the six of us struggled to pull her out. She was an extremely heavy woman and not at all pleased with her nephews for allowing this to happen. She refused to visit again until the project that she called "our waterworks" was completed—and she never let them forget that they had tried to "do her in," as she put it.

John and Nellie Harris came each night to peer into the hole to "see who you caught today."

After two weeks, the hole was finished, along with the trenches for installing the pipes and electrical cords. Donald's check arrived and we were notified that the rest of our plumbing supplies were ready to be picked up. We were jubilant and celebrated with a barely affordable steak supper and a bottle of cheap wine. We invited John and Nellie to join us.

Dream on! Bad luck was not finished with us yet! That night the rains came. Torrents of water poured out of the sky for three days. Covered with boards and tarpaper, the hole still filled with mud. Ignoring the downpour that threatened to drown them while they packed, Donald's family left for their duty in Michigan's Upper Peninsula, where they would spend the summer living in an old Army tent in the county park. ("Great promotion," Hazel laughed. "At least here we had a roof over our heads. Now we'll have to hold an umbrella over our heads all night." They knew the tent leaked.)

When the rain stopped, we dipped the mud out of the hole with buckets. And when Donald's family visited on their way home that fall, we treated them all to a bath in our new bathroom.

Every time I turn on a faucet, I say a little prayer of thanksgiving. What luxuries we take for granted today! What changes we have watched in our long lives! Donald became the head of the State Sanitation Board for South Dakota. He died of Lou Gehrig's disease in 1978. Hazel lives in Minnesota in an assisted-living home. Our children laugh when we reminisce about "our waterworks" during our Good Old Days. We call those days the best days of our lives. ❖

A Whole Lot of Rocking

By Ann Oliver

It was the year 1946, and the radio was blasting out a new song. Unlike the melancholy tunes like *I'll Walk Alone*, it was a happy song about our boys coming home to the wives and sweethearts they had left behind:

Kiss me once then kiss me twice
Then kiss me once again.
It's been a long, long time.

The song, *It's Been a Long Time* was about the couples who had stood before the preacher, or perhaps a justice of the peace, and said those vows before he marched away … she in her dress with a corsage and little hat with a veil, and he in his uniform, standing so proud and tall. Those words "until death do us part" took on a whole new meaning during those war-torn years.

My cousin Toby was one of those who had said her vows during World War II. She had gone to Temple, Texas, where her brother Elmer was stationed at a nearby Army base to visit him and his wife. When she and her sister-in-law went to the mess hall to see her brother, who was an Army cook, she felt someone staring at her as they walked across the hall. She looked up into the big brown eyes of a young soldier who was doing KP duty. He was peeling potatoes and humming a gospel song. Their eyes met for a moment and then she moved on.

After the girls left, the young soldier called out to his friend Elmer, "Who was the cute girl?"

"Why, that was my wife," Elmer replied.

"Funny guy," Ted said. "I meant the *other* cute girl."

"Oh, her. That is my little sister who is staying with us."

"Well," Ted announced, "I am going home with you tonight."

Elmer's wife, Vera, loved to cook and had soldiers in every night for cake or pie and coffee. But it was not these sweets that Ted was after. He wanted to get to know that cute little sister better—and he did. In fact, Toby made a monumental decision after that night. She decided to come live with Elmer and Vera and work at Scott and White hospital at Temple. And so the courtship began.

It wasn't long before wedding bells were ringing and the happy bride and groom moved into an apartment filled with other soldiers and their wives.

The war ended. Toby and Ted moved to Tyler, Texas, where she worked in a department store and he started school on the GI Bill. Then one day, Toby went to the doctor, who told her the news that they were going to increase their family—not by one, but by two! They were going to have twins! The baby boom had started.

A wide-eyed Toby looked at Ted and said, "Oh, Ted, we are going to have twins. What will we do?"

A big grin spread over his face. "A whole lot of rocking!" he answered. And a whole lot of rocking it was, too!

Since all of their parents lived too far away to help, Ted and Toby moved across the street from my family so that Mother could help with the twins. (I did a whole lot of rocking, too.) They rented a room with kitchen privileges and shared the bath with a widow lady. Then the fun began. Remember, this was before disposable diapers; Toby washed all those diapers by hand and hung them out to dry.

But the day came when Ted finished his schooling and got a better job. Then they were able to rent a small house and get a much-needed washing machine. Oh, happy day! Later, when the twins were older and the economy was better, they bought a nice home and continued their happy life.

And it all started when a young soldier saw a cute young girl from Texas at his Army base during World War II. When their eyes met for the first time, love blossomed, and a young couple started an incredible journey together that lasted for nearly 60 years. ❖

MATERNITY WARD

JOHN HYDE
PHILLIPS

Two Cents Apiece

By D. A. Guiliani

During the school year, I studied, read and played, but in summer I was resourceful. At age 8, in 1950, I helped my dad pick at a potato farm on Labor Day weekend for the first time. I made $3 for two days' work—great money back then. And the next summer, I picked up pop bottles along the highway on the south end of town, collecting them in a brown paper bag. Then I brought them to our neighborhood grocery store where I was paid two cents apiece for them. My Mr. Peanut green plastic bank grew heavy.

I could earn a more reliable two cents apiece, however, delivering our local daily newspaper.

My neighbor had a three-street route that totaled 99 papers. He walked them door-to-door, Monday through Friday. But on Saturdays, the paperboy jobbed out the route to his little brother and me. He was 7 and I was 9.

We picked up the bundled papers at Ewald's store, a neighborhood grocery in Iron Mountain, Mich., on East D Street. Then we walked to G Street where the route began. Each of us carried half the load. I took one side of the street and Don took the other.

The ink on those black-and-white pages blackened our hands when we folded the papers to stick them between the screened and main doors. No one allowed us to just toss the papers in the yard, although a few customers let us drop the paper at the foot of the screened door on the porch.

I picked up pop bottles along the highway on the south end of town, collecting them in a brown paper bag. Then I brought them to our neighborhood grocery store where I was paid two cents apiece for them.

Up G, down H, up I and we were finished. From the pickup at Ewald's to the end of I Street, it was a two-hour job.

But that was the work. Next came the incredible pleasure. We hiked up steep Park Avenue from the end of East I Street, cut through Gendron's yard and entered Blackhall's yard.

Mr. Blackhall was a big baseball fan. So were we. We played the game every afternoon all summer, except during pouring rain. We had one ball and one bat. What else could you need? Oh, yeah—gloves. The pitcher and catcher got to use the two gloves that were to be found in the neighborhood. Everyone else used their bare hands to catch grounders and pop-ups.

We were one big collection of Detroit Tiger fans, living 500 miles north of the pros in Briggs Stadium. We listened to the games on radio if our mothers didn't push us outside. But on Saturdays, that wasn't a problem.

The papers came to Ewald's early on Saturday—at noon, not 3 o'clock, as they did on weekdays. By the time we got to Blackhall's, we were tired, sweaty and hungry. In Mr. Blackhall's front yard were two yellow transparent apple trees. They were the first apples of the season to mature—sweet, mellow and soft—two months ahead of Cortlands and Delicious.

And tied to the two trees was a tan, string mesh hammock. We were never clear as to who actually used the hammock. It was always empty when we entered the yard.

The main door to the Blackhall house was

Returning Bottles for Refund by Amos Sewell © 1959 SEPS: Licensed by Curtis Publishing

open, the screen door was in place, and the Tiger game was blaring into the yard from the radio. Mr. Blackhall was lying on the couch, shoes off, white sleeveless T-shirt and dark pants in place.

The first time we stopped, we actually went to the door to ask, but that was the sole formality. After that initial stop, we simply stretched out on the hammock, one of us on each end, and yelled, "Mr. Blackhall, may we have an apple?"

"Ya." Why talk when you can listen to the game? We'd reach up and pluck a yellow orb from a branch, rub it on a sleeve and bite.

Every Saturday, like clockwork, we delivered the papers and hightailed it to Blackhall's for baseball and an apple. No summer has been that easy since. You grow up, you get real jobs, you have to pay for your own hammock, you mow the grass under it and prune the apple trees. I had no idea what generosity Mr. Blackhall had in letting us use his hammock and eat his apples. He never said no, and he never yelled, two conditions that really matter with kids. And every time, of course, I had earned two cents apiece for the papers I delivered. ❖

Baby Boomer Memories

By Donna McGuire Tanner

How lucky am I? I was born in 1947, so I am fortunate enough to be a member of the elite group known as baby boomers.

The kids of my generation journeyed through childhood blissfully, unaware of the harsh years that had just preceded our births.

My older brother, Danny, and I were gifted with a time when we were only fenced in by the limits of our imaginations as we invented games to play and entertained ourselves. Television was just something we had heard other people talking about.

I remember when it happened. It was February 1953. We lived in the small community of Weirwood, W.Va.

Danny's friend Richard asked if we wanted to watch a program called *Howdy Doody* on his aunt and uncle's television set. Our mother, Rachel, readily agreed because they lived right next-door to us.

It is etched forever in my memory. We three kids seated ourselves cross-legged in front of the big brown box with a window. My brother and I were in awe of this "radio with a movie picture."

When Buffalo Bob Smith, the host of the program, shouted, "Say kids! What time is it?" the children in the studio audience—the Peanut Gallery—shouted back, "It's Howdy Doody Time!" Even at 5 years old, I realized at that moment that something in my life had changed.

A few days later, a furniture-store truck pulled up to our house. It was a surprise for his family. My father, Basil, was a West Virginia coal miner. He could not really afford the Admiral television set that was being delivered, so he had bought it "on time." He had heard Danny and me talking excitedly about *Howdy Doody*, and so it was

that he wanted to please us. And please us he did!

Every evening found us, brother and sister (and later our younger sister, Brenda), in front of *our* Admiral. After the program, Mom would snap off the set and outside we would flee to once more free our creative young minds to create new games.

I am from a place in time where there is a misty gray line of when we were the generation before *and* after television, as it gradually drifted into our lives.

I am lucky, and so glad to be able to call myself a baby boomer. ❖

Clarabelle the Clown, left; Bob Smith, center and Howdy Doody performing at a taping of The Howdy Doody Show. Photo by Martha Holmes Circa 1948. Time Life Pictures/ Getty Images

A Time When Dreams Came True

By Verla A. Mooth

During World War II, I was employed at a large Army camp close to my parents' home in the Ozark Mountains of southwestern Missouri. I worked in the office of the sales officer where supplies of food were purchased and distributed to the soldiers. In the early part of December 1942, a newly arrived soldier from Chicago was assigned to our office to work with me. We worked together for a year, then started to date and fell in love. We were married on Sept. 5, 1944.

When Camp Crowder was constructed, an influx of some 55,000 soldiers, workers and their families flooded into our area. It was almost impossible to secure housing of any kind. My new husband and I were obliged to start house-keeping in a one-room cottage. All we could do was dream of the day when the war would be over and we could go to Chicago and have a better home. My new husband had worked as a salesman for a natural sponge and chamois company before he was drafted. He knew that his job was waiting for him when he returned.

The war ended, and my husband was finally released from the service in February 1946. Russ had called his parents, who lived in the Hyde Park area of Chicago, to be looking for an apartment for us. But all their searching was futile. Soldiers were returning home by the thousands, many bringing new wives with them. There wasn't even a sleeping room to be found.

Finally it was decided that we would have to stay with his parents in their apartment. This was fine for my husband, for he started back to work within a few days. I decided that I would go back to work also. Jobs were plentiful, and I had no trouble finding work. I secured a job with the 5th Army Headquarters in Chicago. But the dream of a home of my own had to be put aside for the time being.

Another dream was failing to be answered. I longed to be a mother, but after an examination at the Lying-In Hospital, which was connected with the University of Chicago, I was told that I could never bear a child. I wanted to adopt a baby, but my husband said we should wait until we had a home of our own.

Finally, in the fall of 1947, we were able to secure a large, six-room, two-flat apartment through the recommendation of our pastor. The landlord lived in the lower flat. We furnished our apartment with all-new furniture: coordinating drapes and sofa and chair covers, which were custom-ordered. My dreams were finally starting to come true.

I was now working as a secretary and in youth ministry at the First Church of the Nazarene, where we attended. Everyone thought we were a happy young couple. But as our fourth anniversary approached, I longed for a baby with every fiber of my being. I had gone through painful procedures to try to become pregnant, but to no avail.

My husband finally realized that being a mother was the most important thing in my life. In July 1948, he consented to go with me to the Chicago Foundlings Home and file an application to adopt a baby. I continued working, and in mid-December, the home called and said they were coming to our apartment to see our home. The Christmas tree was all decorated and everything was spotless.

Things moved quickly after that, and we were asked to come to the Home on Jan. 29, 1949, to see our new baby. When a tiny, 10-week-old baby boy was laid in my arms, I thought my heart would burst with love and happiness. The baby cooed and smiled at me, and I baptized his tiny body with my tears of gratitude.

My husband was allowed to hold him for a while, and then we were informed that we could take him home on Feb. 3. I spent the next three days shopping for baby furniture and baby clothes. We had made arrangements with the landlord to pay more rent for the extra water we used, but they were not really happy about our new baby. But Feb. 3 was the happiest day of my life. I was a mother. Never again would my arms be empty.

I had quit work the day before the baby was brought home. We named our precious baby boy Loren Dirk. Now each day was filled to overflowing with household chores, and playing with and caring for Dirk. I loved to bathe and dress the baby, and feed and hold him. I rejoiced in each new accomplishment. Before I realized it, my baby was an 18-month-old toddler. It was time for a new home with a yard for him to grow up in.

My husband's work took him away from home part of the time, so I asked my father-in-law to take me out to a nearby suburb to look at a house I had seen advertised in the Sunday paper. It was a chilly April afternoon when I first saw the house that was to be the fulfillment of my dreams. It was on an unpaved street, and about half of the lots were still vacant. Five new homes were under construction on that same block.

When we walked into the spacious living room, a fire was burning in the natural fireplace. I could see clear through the hall and out the dining-room window into a large back yard. The house was six years old and had five rooms. My father-in-law went into the basement and looked at the construction of the house. On the way home, he assured me that it had been built just before the war started and was well constructed. I called Russ that night and he agreed that we could buy the house as soon as he returned.

And so it was that in June 1950 we moved to the village of Evergreen Park, Ill., where I was to raise my family and spend the next 30 years of my life. Almost every morning we were awakened by the sound of a bulldozer breaking ground for a new home. The new houses were quickly sold to returning GIs with small children.

In December 1951, we were again favored by God and allowed to adopt a baby girl on the morning of Christmas Eve. We named her Paula. As a stay-at-home mother, I found great happiness in keeping a spotless home, doing all the things a mother and wife does, and relishing my children's every accomplishment. There were hours of watching TV, with excellent programs such as *Captain Kangaroo* and Miss Francis and her *Ding-Dong School*. There was swimming, Cub Scouts, Brownies, school activities and church.

During the 1950s, our village grew at an amazing speed. Three new grade schools were built, one just two blocks from us, as well as a public high school, two Catholic high schools and a college. Within a block of our home we had a grocery store, gift shop, beauty shop and a barber shop. One of the first large shopping malls in the country was built just a mile from our home. It was a safe and secure place to raise a family. We added three rooms to our house in 1955. To say that it was a time of growth and expansion was an understatement! It was the best of times and the best of places to be alive and raising a family. And, oh, how swiftly the years flew by!

Before I had time to realize it, my husband was no longer with me. Dirk was married and had a family and was living in Florida. Paula was also married and living in Missouri, where I grew up. On Nov. 17, 1985, I walked through my home one last time. The moving van had already taken all my furniture. I wiped the tears from my eyes and walked out the back door for the last time. I felt so empty and alone, as if a part of me was being left behind.

As I pulled out of the driveway of 9835 St. Louis Ave. and headed to my new home near my daughter, I felt lonely. But I knew I was not alone, for I was taking with me all my cherished memories of the time and place where I had spent the best years of my life. ❖

And Baby Makes Three

Just over a month after World War II ended in 1945, *It's Been a Long Time* hit No. 1 on the Billboard charts. Performed by Bing Crosby and accompanied by Les Paul on the guitar, the song captured the joy and anticipation of young love about to be fulfilled. The song, written and composed by Sammy Cahn and Jule Styne, would remain on the charts for 16 weeks.

It's Been a Long Time

Kiss me once, then kiss me twice
Then kiss me once again.
It's been a long, long time.
Haven't felt like this, my dear
Since I can't remember when.
It's been a long, long time

You'll never know how many dreams
I've dreamed about you.
Or just how empty they all seemed without you.
So kiss me once, then kiss me twice
Then kiss me once again.
It's been a long, long time.

Ah, kiss me once, then kiss me twice
Then kiss me once again.
It's been a long time.
Haven't felt like this my dear
Since I can't remember when
It's been a long, long time.

You'll never know how many dreams
I've dreamed about you.
Or just how empty they all seemed without you.
So kiss me once, then kiss me twice
Then kiss me once again.
It's been a long, long time.
Long, long time.

Even though *My Blue Heaven* was made popular first in the 1920s when recorded by the great Rudy Vallee, a recording by Fats Domino gave Boomers and their parents a reminder that heaven can be "just Mollie and me, and baby makes three." The music was composed by Walter Donaldson, with words by George Whiting.

My Blue Heaven

Day is ending, birds are wending
Back to the shelter of each little nest they love.
Nightshades falling, lovebirds calling.
What makes the world go round?
Nothing but love.

When Whippoorwills call,
And ev'ning is nigh,
We'll hurry to my blue heaven.
A turn to the right
A little white light
Will lead you to my blue heaven.

You'll see a smiling face, a fireplace,
A cozy room,
A little nest that's nestled where
The roses bloom.

Just Mollie and me
And baby makes three;
We're happy in my blue heaven.

You'll see a smiling face, a fireplace,
A cozy room,
A little nest that's nestled where
The roses bloom.

Just Mollie and me
And baby makes three;
We're happy in my blue heaven.
We're happy in my blue heaven. ❖